D1288805

BRANCH LINES
of the
SOUTHERN RAILWAY

Volume Two

by

George Reeve & Chris Hawkins

WILD SWAN PUBLICATIONS LTD.

© Wild Swan Publications Ltd. and George Reeve & Chris Hawkins 1983
ISBN 0 906867 14 2

FOR 'SMOKEY'

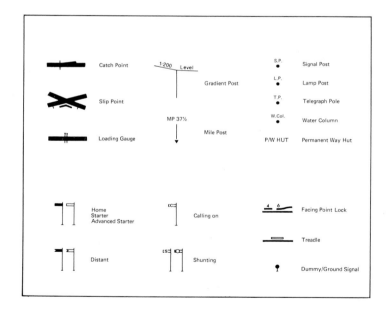

Designed by Paul Karau
Typesetting by Berkshire Publishing Services
Photo reproduction and offset plates by Oxford Litho Plates Ltd.
Printed by Thomas Leach Ltd., Abingdon

Published by
WILD SWAN PUBLICATIONS LTD.,
Hopgoods Farm Cottage, Upper Bucklebury, Berks.

Contents

Introduction vii

THE BANSTEAD AND EPSOM DOWNS RAILWAY 1
    Sutton 2
    Belmont 13
    Banstead 19
    Epsom Downs 29
    Locomotives & operational details 39
    Architectural plans and elevations 43

THE LYDD RAILWAY (*The New Romney and Dungeness Branches*) . . . 49
    Appledore 53
    Brookland 57
    Lydd 63
    Dungeness 71
    Lydd-on-Sea 76
    Greatstone-on-Sea 78
    New Romney 81
    Locomotives & operational details 91
    Architectural plans and elevations 94

THE AXMINSTER & LYME REGIS LIGHT RAILWAY 97
    Axminster 104
    Combpyne 121
    Lyme Regis 131
    Locomotives & operational details 146
    Architectural plans and elevations 150

Acknowledgements 152

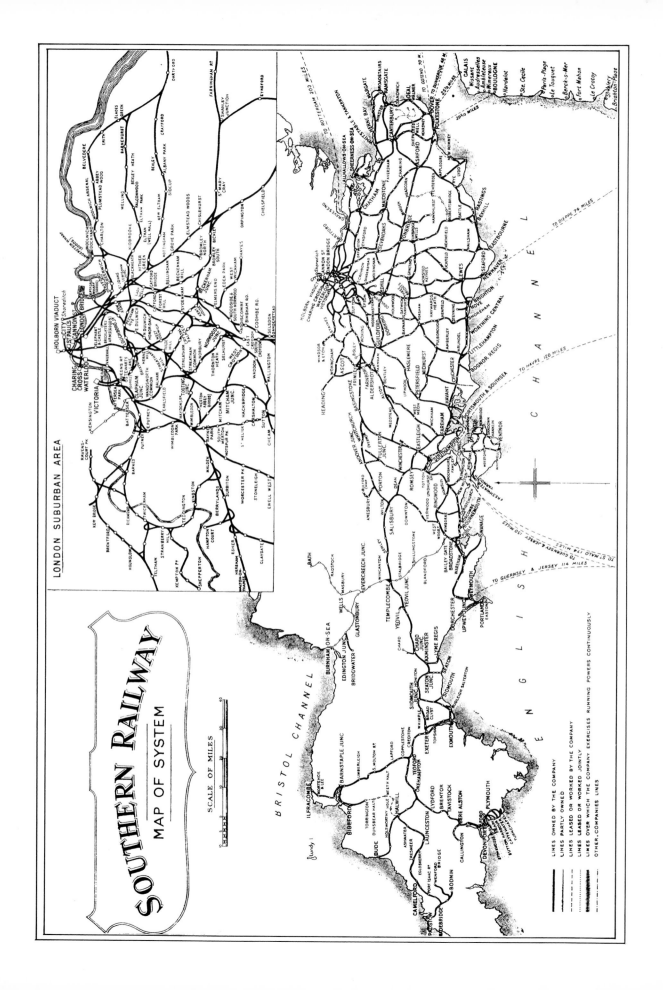

Combpyne on 7th July 1959.   *H. C. Casserley*

Introduction

Completing a pair of volumes, this work deals with three further branch lines of the former Southern Railway. Again there is a representative from each of the company's three main constituents, the South Eastern and Chatham Railway, the London Brighton and South Coast Railway and the London and South Western Railway.

One line, remarkably, is still open, drawn into the growing capital many years ago and sustained since by (dwindling) commuter traffic. The future of the Epsom Downs line is now far from secure and lies shadowed in uncertainty. The two remaining lines tell a more conventional, if sadder, tale, the best known being the spiralling, soaring wonder of the Lyme Regis branch. Its clattering trains, laden with holidaymakers, echoed through the woods and across the downs above Lyme, proclaiming a way of life doomed in the post-war world. On the South Coast, far from the rolling hills of Lyme, wandered a different sort of branch altogether. The bold few who ventured beyond Lydd were destined for chalet or caravan rather than a West Country hotel. The journey could hold an equal fascination, nevertheless, though such delights, across featureless flats or chalkland heights, are now long lost. Utterly sundered from us now, it is hoped that some distant echo at least might sound through these pages.

Again the detailed drawings are from original contract material and all of the track plans are reproduced at a scale of 2 chains to one inch and most of the structures at 2mm to one foot. Uniform scales have been used to show comparative sizes of locations and structures and, whilst the scales were obviously chosen primarily to suit the restricted space available, the more popular modelling scale of 4mm to one foot can be arrived at simply by doubling the dimensions shown.

George Reeve and Chris Hawkins

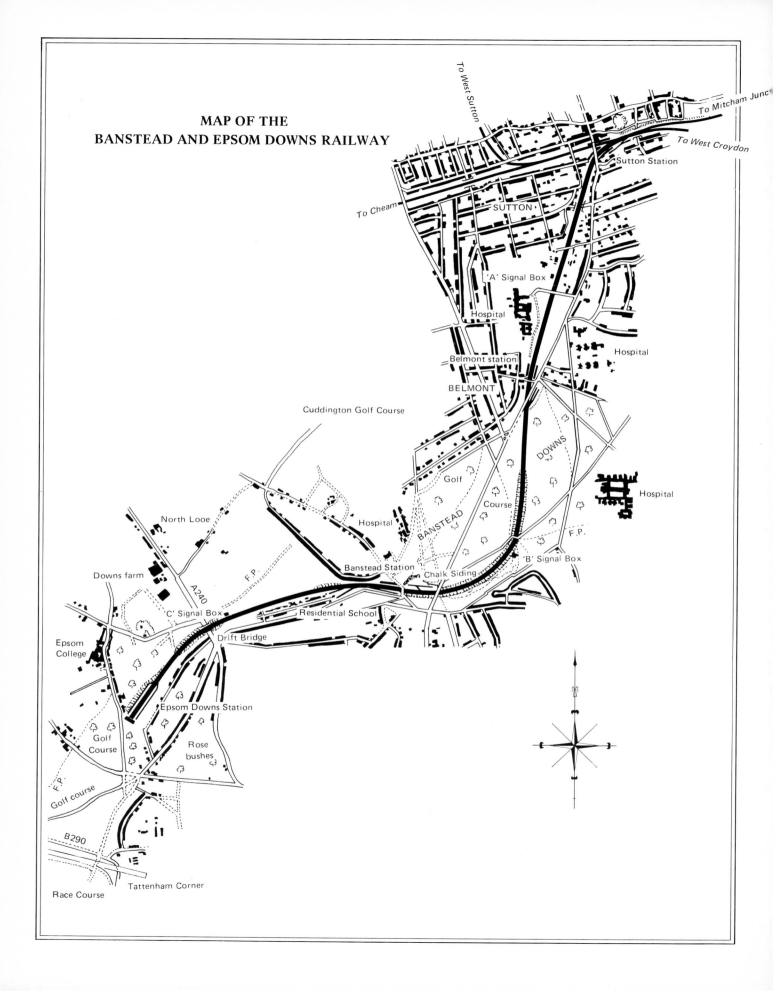

MAP OF THE
BANSTEAD AND EPSOM DOWNS RAILWAY

To West Sutton

To Mitcham Junc

To West Croydon

Sutton Station

To Cheam

SUTTON

'A' Signal Box

Hospital

Hospital

Belmont station

BELMONT

Cuddington Golf Course

DOWNS

Golf

Hospital

Course

North Looe

BANSTEAD

F.P.

Hospital

F.P.

'B' Signal Box

Downs farm

A240

F.P.

Banstead Station

Chalk Siding

'C' Signal Box

Residential School

Epsom
College

Drift Bridge

Epsom Downs Station

Golf
Course

Rose
bushes

F.P.

Golf course

B290

Tattenham Corner

Race Course

The Banstead and Epsom Downs Railway

THIS was closest to London of the lines described and differs from the others in several important respects. It was included in the Southern's electrification programme, it is overwhelmingly a commuter line, and most importantly is still open!

It was built with a very particular traffic in mind and became one of a unique group of railways specifically serving racecourses.

The line straggled across the sparsely populated, rather bleak North Downs and at one time the 'Chatham' had cast their eyes over the route, going so far as to formulate a bill for a line to the racecourse. A series of negotiations followed and the London Chatham & Dover Railway eventually withdrew, a nominally independent company under Brighton tutelage receiving authority to build the line on 17th July 1862. Thus was the Banstead and Epsom Downs Railway Act passed, in 1862, with a capital of £85,000. Within days the Board had appointed a Captain L. Flower as engineer to the line with a Mr. Shrimpton as contractor. He prepared two separate schemes, the second being accepted by the directors who set the completion date (optimistically, in the event) of the contract at 1st November 1863.

Things, it seems, did not go too well and in the next few months something of a 'palace coup' was carried out amongst the management of the company. There was a reshuffle of directors in June 1863 and a barrister, Mr. F. Dale, took over as engineer in charge of the new work. There is reference to a Mr. Charles Garrett as a successor to Mr. Shrimpton but only a year or so previously the company had been complaining of 'the unwarranted interference of a man named Garrett'. An awful tangle ensued and by 1864 Garrett in a rejoinder was claiming six months payment at the astonishing rate of £1,000 per week. Squabbles and injunctions leading even to scuffles followed and by February 1864 a third contractor was being actively sought.

On 30th June 1864 the Board reviewed its finances and was pleased to report that receipts so far slightly exceeded expenditure. They had sold 8,500 shares worth £47,900 and had spent so far only £47,815, made up of £25,060 for work and materials, £5,255 for land and compensation, and an incredible £17,500 on 'preliminary and parlimentary charges'. A special meeting of 19th December 1864 resolved that the company amalgamate with the LBSCR and the line, completed by the aptly named Messrs. Faithful and Son, eventually opened for traffic on 22nd May 1865.

Pre-electrification scene at Epsom Downs terminus on 18th December 1926.   *H. C. Casserley*

1

2

SUTTON

The first station at Sutton opened with the line from West Croydon to Epsom Town on 10th May 1847. Of rather less than substantial construction, in wood, it was deemed inadequate for the junction of the new Epsom Downs branch and a much larger building arose some distance to the west. On completion in May 1865 the original station was abandoned, its site eventually comprising part of the substantial Sutton goods yard. The original 1847 building now serves as a pavilion for Sutton Cricket Club.

The new station stood in a cutting and contemporary engravings show it, when new, to have had an air of the Italianate about it. The top part, under a flat hipped roof, was devoted to the station master and his family, who enjoyed three large bedrooms, with kitchen, scullery, etc. below. Passengers passed through an entrance at road level, by the bridge, and descended to the station proper below. Here was the general waiting room and ticket office, with porters' room and a coal store behind. In front of the station building and obscured here but for a few chimneys, was the parcels office/store, ornate and colonnaded. Before the main platform canopies were constructed (the last, in the branch bay, it will be seen, was nearing completion only in 1882) a single high verandah, about 10 ft wide, led at right angles from the building to the station edge. The whole had a distinctly 'Venetian' air. The date quoted for this photograph is 1882, the year in which complete remodelling of the 1865 station began. Platform 1, on the right, underwent considerable cutting back as part of this scheme. *Collection D. Brough*

Sutton station grew steadily in importance although the branch itself contributed little traffic, even race day patronage proving something of a disappointment. Wholly absorbed by the LBSCR even before it opened, the line at first had a daily service of eight trains each way, the four provided on Sundays soon being withdrawn. The Downs were still lonely and sparsely inhabited, but Sutton found itself increasingly part of the spreading metropolis. Suburban services from Sutton thus flourished, especially so since an alternative London route had opened, via Mitcham Junction, in October 1868. By 1882, therefore, further alterations were being embarked upon. A new booking hall and ticket office was built, spanning the cutting, alongside part of the preceding station building. At the far end of the new building, recorded here about 1916, was a new gentlemen's waiting room. *Courtesy Sutton Library*

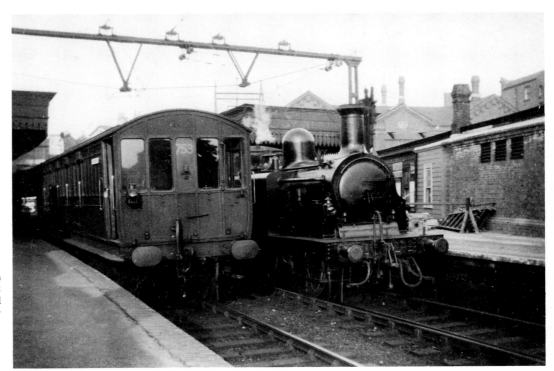

An Epsom Downs motor train at Sutton, with No. B282 alongside Platform 3 in April 1928.   *H. F. Wheeller*

4

The branch was included in the wholesale electrification of the Southern Railway era and, following a tour of inspection by the General Manager and a number of senior officers in the early part of 1927, electrification work began. Electric services replaced steam on the branch from 17th June 1928, with a generous half-hourly service from London Bridge, seven days a week. A wholly new station, to cater adequately for these modern services, opened for traffic in 1928, the previous clutter of varying generations giving way to a tiled hipped roof building bearing the ubiquitous motif 'Frequent Electric Trains . . . etc.'
Lens of Sutton

The newly opened station in 1928. The wide, spacious footbridge constructed behind this building was known as 'The Gallery'.
Courtesy Sutton Library

The tall starting signals on Platform 1 provided an admirable viewpoint from which the station layout (and the new 'Gallery') could be seen to advantage, as in this view of about 1929. The water column had disappeared by 1950, and had itself replaced a water tank on Platform 4. It was succeeded by a 'parachute' tank.

The late E. Wallis

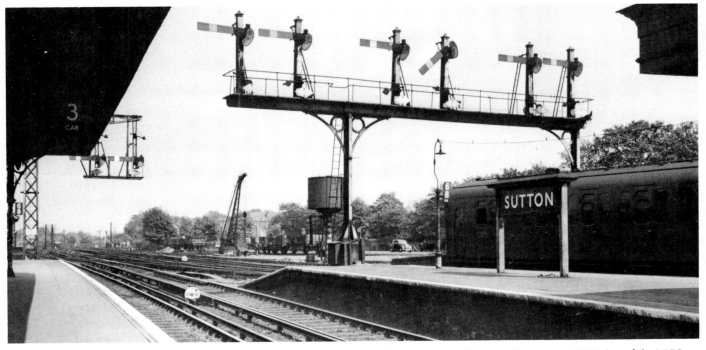

The Epsom Downs branch was notable for a wealth of interesting signals and Sutton too could boast a fine array. A 1950 view of the LBSC pattern lower quadrant erected by the Southern Railway shortly after Grouping. This carried the 'up' starting signals for platforms 2, 3 and 4.

D. Clayton

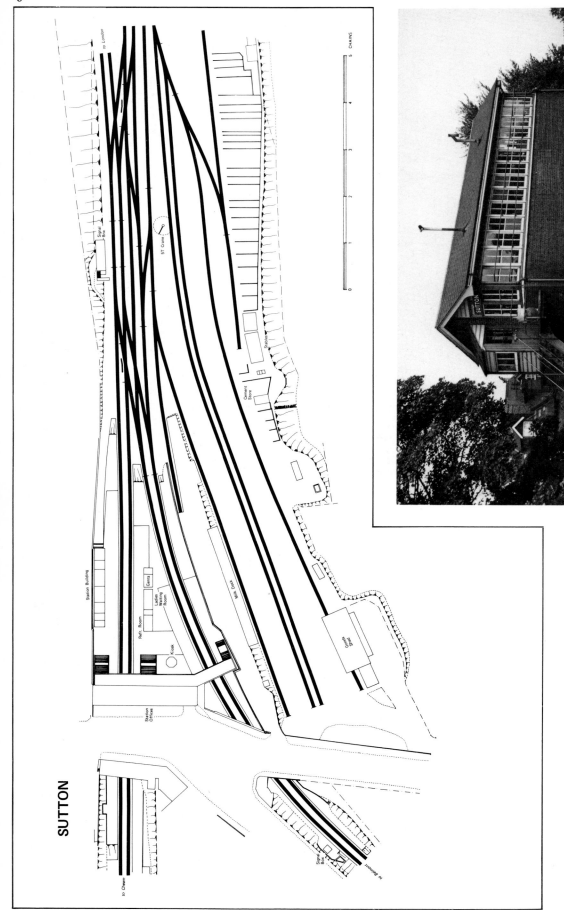

SUTTON

to London

Signal Box

5T Crane

Station Building

Refr. Room

Gents

Ladies Waiting Room

Kiosk

Station Offices

Milk Dock

Cement Store

Stables

Goods Shed

to Cheam

Signal Box

to Belmont

CHAINS

0 1 2 3 4 5

Sutton Junction signal box in 1967. The Southern moved it to this
new site, at the London end of the station, in 1925.
J. Scrace

The Platform 1 starter provides another fine view towards London, a push-pull set standing in the goods yard. The principal commodity dealt with was coal for domestic use. There was formerly a siding on the 'up' side, its head shunt visible under the AC overhead electrification gantry. The 'siding' is considered by some to have once been used by Wimbledon motors though the absence of a facing point lock casts doubt on this notion. It was never electrified.

The late E. Wallis

An 'E4' 0—6—2T, No. 2498, shunts the yard in 1938.

H. F. Wheeller

Sutton in 1951 with the branch platforms to the left.   *D. Clayton*

Sutton West signal box at the country end of the station in the 1950s. The spare ground was formerly occupied by three carriage sidings, a fourth running alongside the 'down' main line.

Lens of Sutton

Stewarts Lane mogul No. 31409 standing on the 'down' branch line. Trains could leave in either direction, from either of the branch platforms.

Lens of Sutton

'D1' 0–4–2T No. B269 at Sutton beneath the A.C. overhead wires, on 24th May 1926. There were some through trains off the branch at this time, the only regular 'up' working being the 9.10 a.m. ex-Epsom Downs all stations to Victoria (except Battersea Park), routed via the 'up' main line from Streatham Junction. There was a quick turn round at Victoria and the same engine and coaches worked back as the 10.23 ex-Victoria and Epsom Downs arriving at 11.16. This train consisted of the 'D1' loco, rail motor set and a set of seven 6-wheeled coaches kept at Epsom Downs.

A.C. electric trains started to run to Sutton from Victoria via Selhurst and West Croydon in 1925. Overhead wiring was fixed on the 'down' branch line, to allow 10-coach overhead electrics to clear the crossover. They would then reverse into Platform 3 ready for return to Victoria. This only happened three or four times a day when Platform 4 was required for through motor trains to the branch. The headcode carried was:

9
Sutton via Selhurst

Trains to Sutton consisted of electric locos sandwiched between two trailers. Two of these sets were used in rush hours, but the A.C. system was gradually run down, the last train running on 21st September 1929.   *H. C. Casserley*

The Brighton Road bridge crossing the branch platforms.   *L & GRP*

A diminutive ground frame cabin set into the 'up' platform controlled some movements on the branch at Sutton. Provided with twelve levers, it was built in 1916 and replaced an eight lever example dating from 1878. The latter, measuring 8 ft 3 ins x 9 ft 6 ins, was controlled from Sutton Junction box and stood on the same site. The 1916 box closed on 30th July 1969, when colour light signalling was installed. The lower quadrant signal replaced an old LBSC bracket signal.   *D. Clayton*

'A' INTERMEDIATE   c.1900 signalling diagram

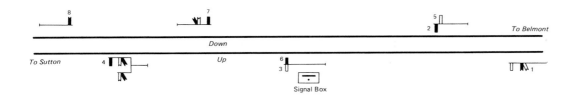

The line's extraordinary and brief traffic 'peaks' resulted in one of its most interesting features, small 'intermediate' signal boxes, their purpose being to shorten the block sections. Intended solely for race day use (latterly only on the occasion of the 'Derby' and the 'Oaks') three such intermediate block cabins were built. They came into use around 1900 and were known as 'A', 'B' and 'C' respectively, 'A' box being sited between Sutton and Belmont, 1,408 yards from Sutton Junction box. The signal arms were stored in the respective boxes throughout most of the year and were only fixed on the posts a week or so before required. Testing was normally carried out on the eve of the event. Used only during daylight hours, no lamps or spectacle plates were necessary. 'A' intermediate box is shown on 5th June 1924 with relief signalman, H. Richardson in charge. Sutton Junction's 'up' fixed distant on the branch (which also carried the 'A' intermediate starting signal) was reputed to be one of only two on the LBSC, the other being on the 'Cuckoo Line'.   *The late E. Wallis and D. Clayton*

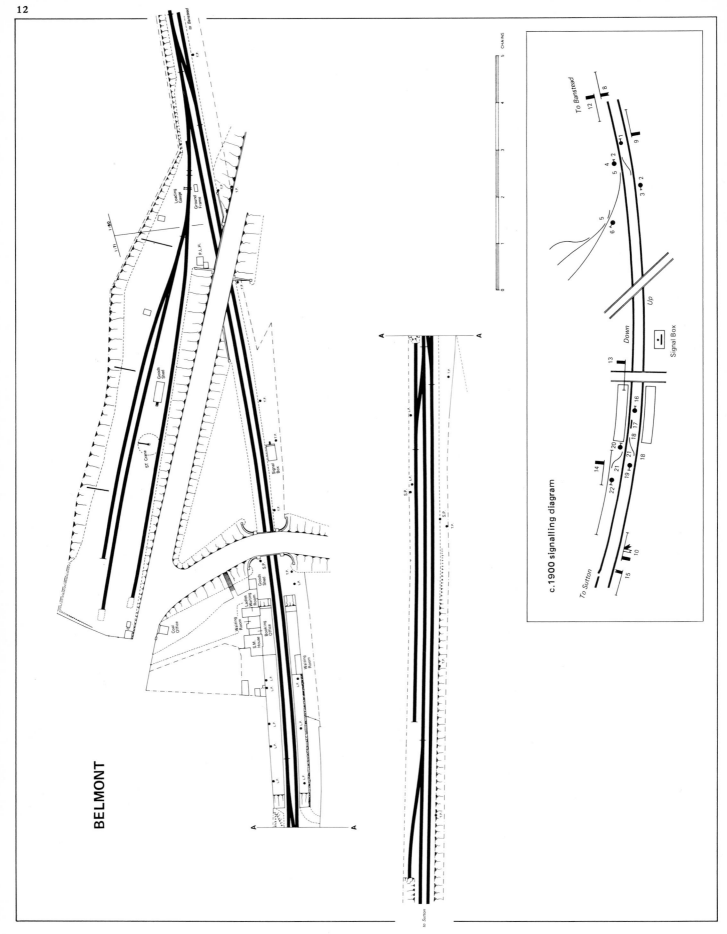

12

BELMONT

to Sutton

to Banstead

Loading Gauge

Ground Frame

P.L.H.

Goods Shed

5T Crane

Signal Box

Goods Shed

Coal Office

Waiting Room

Ladies Waiting Room

Booking Office

S.M. House

Waiting Room

1 in 80

1 in 71

A · · · · A

S.P.

S.P.

to Sutton

CHAINS

0 1 2 3 4 5

c.1900 signalling diagram

To Banstead

To Sutton

Down

Up

Signal Box

12

8

1

9

2

4

5

3

2

5

6

13

14

15

10

16

17

18

18

19

20

21

22

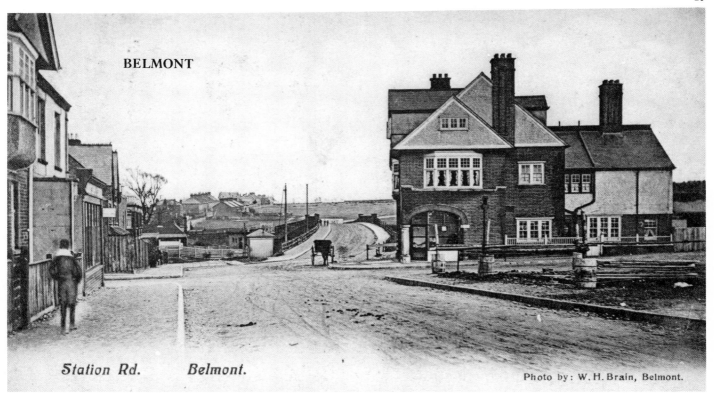

BELMONT

Station Rd.   Belmont.

Photo by: W.H.Brain, Belmont.

Station Road, Belmont, prior to 1927. Housing development was by now at an advanced stage. This view clearly shows the position of the original level crossing and the diversion to the bridge which replaced it.   *W. H. Brain, courtesy Ted Crawforth*

Belmont in LBSCR days, still very much a rural byway. 'Belmont, Banstead & Epsom Downs, fast to Belmont' was the ironic cry of one guard on the pre-electrification motors. Part of a long tradition of gentle railway humour, he was a Brighton man who had lost the sight of an eye. Affectionately known as 'Nelson', he was periodically blinded by soot while looking out of his van window.   *Lens of Sutton*

Belmont in the early years. The name was popular in such entrepreneurial schemes launched into sparsely populated areas. The larger gabled portion of the building formed the station master's house, with kitchen, scullery and sitting room at ground level and two bedrooms above. The booking hall was entered through the central porchway, with the ticket office on the right and waiting room on the left. Prior to improvements carried out in 1904, the public part of the building was simply two waiting rooms with a small booking office at the side. The wooden building bearing the legend 'Liptons Tea' served as the goods shed. *Lens of Sutton*

Station and train staff pose behind a Sutton bound motor train with 'Terrier' No. 66. The 'LV' plate denoted the 'Last Vehicle'. The early LBSC system for driving the locomotive from a trailer coach was by means of levers and chains. 'Terrier' class engines were only fitted at the bunker end and the whistle was operated by a cord which passed through the tube carrying strap handles for standing passengers. Some 'D1' class engines were also fitted, but they had the control gear at both ends and usually operated with the engine sandwiched between two driving trailer coaches (See page 40). The engine whistle was operated by a cord from both coaches and a small pulley wheel was attached to the side of the chimney to support the cord from the front coach. The old pulley wheel remained on the chimney of No. 627 until the early 'twenties, long after it was last used. This system of mechanical control was not satisfactory and a new design of compressed air control gear was evolved, operated by the Westinghouse brake compressor. Three air pipes were provided labelled 'storage', 'control' and 'back pressure'. The engine and control cylinder were under the footplate and a rod was fixed vertically up to the right of the regulator handle, the latter a special item with an extension on the right side. When in use for trailer driving, the two were connected by a steel safety chain and, when driving from the engine, the pin was removed, the regulator used by the driver in the cab as usual. Special air operated chime whistles were used, similar to the A.C. electric trains, and operated from the driving trailer cab. Steam engine whistles were retained, the compressed air control system first coming into use in 1912.

Lens of Sutton

The Railway Station Belmont.

Bathurst Sutton Copyright.

A push-pull set enters the station ready for a return working, presumably to Sutton or West Croydon in Brighton days. Villas for the lesser gentry had appeared by about 1910 but residential development did not take place until after the First World War. The milk churns are an indication of the line's still rural nature. Well away from respectable folk was the workhouse, the ugly building overlooking the station. In steam days some difficulty was experienced starting through full length 'down' trains at Belmont, one particular misfortune befalling a suburban set in wet weather. The engine kept slipping and began to roll back towards Sutton. This backward momentum had to be arrested before a derailment occurred at the catch points beyond the refuge siding and the train came to a stand whilst assistance was summoned. After a wait of about 25 minutes, a 2-coach motor train from Sutton arrived with a 'D1' tank leading. It buffered up behind the train and then backed it out of Belmont, the suburban set continuing on its journey without further mishap.

Collection J. Scrace

Belmont in 1961. The name was not actually adopted until 1875, an event noted by few people. The station opened somewhat exotically as 'California' and saw little traffic for very many years. It suffered a direct hit in the bombing of 1940 and the main station building on the 'down' side, was destroyed. Concrete huts were eventually provided by way of replacement but the 'up' side, escaping relatively lightly, retained its structures and canopy. The wooden building dated from 1938 and, rather fortuitously, had rendered the original 'down' side facilities redundant. The new building contained waiting room, ticket office, kiosk, porters' room, etc. The original wooden waiting shelter, cut back some twenty years after opening, is visible as the projection at the far, Sutton, end.

The 'down' platform was extended and raised 'to standard height', and a footbridge, previously at Folkestone Junction, was re-erected at Belmont in 1928 just before electrification. It was to have been extended up to the road bridge, but this particular development was never carried out. Access to the 'up' platform had formerly been by means of a boarded crossing.

D. Thompson

An 'up' motor train approaching Belmont in the 1900s. The bridge, one of two in the vicinity, carries the Brighton Road, whilst the cleared area on the left was the site of the original 1865 goods yard.
Lens of Sutton

Belmont signal box in the 1960s. Opened in 1889, it replaced a box built with the station and located at the country end of the 'up' platform. Of Saxby and Farmer origin, it closed on 21st December 1969, the yard having suffered a similar fate almost a year previously, on 6th January.
J. Scrace

Entry to the new goods yard, opened in 1880, was from the far side of the bridge, along the southern boundary of the Brighton Road. The cramped site of the original yard precluded expansion and it was decided it should be abandoned. The motor service, using 'Terrier' 0—6—0Ts, first ran on 11th June 1906, between West Croydon and Belmont, in competition with suburban electric trams. A siding to stable this unit between workings was proposed at the time, sited on the 'down' side a short distance from the junction of the new yard. In the event it was built at the Sutton end of the station and, known as 'the down lay-by siding', was reported taken out of use on 27th October 1927.
Collection J. Scrace

Belmont yard in March 1936. There was little traffic by this time apart from wagonloads of domestic coal for distribution by Hall & Co.

H. F. Wheeller

0—6—2T No. 2948 quietly simmering in Belmont yard, on 11th October 1935.   *H. F. Wheeller*

18

'I3' 4—4—2T tank No. 2088 approaching Banstead in Southern days. The line took a wide curve to the west between Belmont and Banstead stations, almost the entire length of it contained within a cutting. *Dr. I. C. Allen*

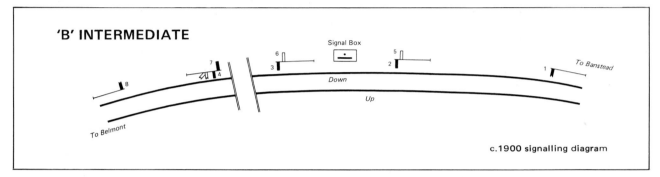

Suggesting more a Forestry Commission watchtower than a signal box, 'B' intermediate stood perched at the top of the cutting. All the frames in these intermediate boxes were of Saxby and Farmer manufacture, the equipment at 'B' cabin being particularly awkward to use. The signalman was forced to step *outside* the box to avoid impaling himself on the up distant lever! Photographed 1949.

D. Clayton and D. J. W. Brough, courtesy G. Hookham

BANSTEAD

Banstead, the next station down the line, was sited within the long cutting, at this point some thirty feet deep. The buildings remained in original condition until the mid-thirties, when, with traffic at last on the increase, various alterations were carried out. The name 'Banstead' bestowed on opening in 1865 was lengthened to 'Banstead and Burgh Heath' on 1st June 1898, reverting to the original following electrification in 1928. The village was a mile or so away uphill and the station remains to this day in a surprisingly rural setting. Its remoteness from what habitation there was in the district meant low receipts for many years. This proved a positive attraction for the kind of institution which seemed to find favour in the nineteenth century, like the 'Kensington and Chelsea' districts school, opened in 1880 to the west of Banstead and served by its own siding. A

similar siding served the South Metropolitan district school near Belmont and in the 1870s the brooding outline of Banstead Lunatic Asylum arose some half a mile to the east of the station. In later years (in somewhat lighter vein) numbers of ramblers came to use the station, attracted by the open downland. The large scale rooftop lettering was obligingly provided by the Southern, to assist pilots making use of Croydon Airport, some miles to the east. The central entrance led into a general waiting room, which occupied the greater part of the building. On the far right was the ticket office and on the left the ladies waiting room and toilet. The attractive detached house formed the station master's residence.

Courtesy Banstead Library

Electrification stimulated traffic and in a general remodelling in 1935 the Southern considerably enlarged and modernized the building. The road-level frontage was little altered, apart from renewal of rotten original windows and the provision of a small shelter over the entrance. A store was built, adjoining the kiosk and a cab hire office built at the opposite end of the building. A large new parcels and ticket office appeared at the rear, practically doubling the floor space. The original ticket office became a bookstall, what remained of the old general waiting room became simply a hallway, whilst the former ladies waiting room was retained.

J. Scrace

Towards Sutton, 2nd June 1924. The small signal was replaced during the 1935 rebuilding work by a larger, bracket apparatus (seen in the picture above). Its new position was even more cramped, requiring a repeater arm beneath, in addition to the bracket. This new SR signal nevertheless retained its 'Brighton' arm, leading to confusion in some subsequent accounts. A track, known as 'Chalk Siding', formerly occupied the spare ground beyond the station arch, to the left, and it was controlled by a ground frame with Annett's Key. After many years of disuse, the area was given over to a local club as a rifle range, the ground frame ('B') officially closing on 10th May 1930. The uninviting door to the right hid a malodorous gents toilet. *The late E. Wallis*

An ignominious end for some 'foreign' wagons at what is reputed to be the 'chalk siding'. *Collection D. Brough, courtesy Derek Clayton*

Banstead platforms in 1961. The new canopies were added during the 1935 scheme, along with improvements to the existing footbridge. The platform extensions, to cater for the new electric sets, can be clearly seen. The 'up' platform was not extended at first and at Epsom Downs passengers for Banstead were warned to use the first three coaches.   *D. Thompson*

'H' class 0—4—4T No. 31521 running through Banstead with a special, 'The South Londoner', on 6th June 1953.   *G. Hookham*

BANSTEAD c.1948 track plan

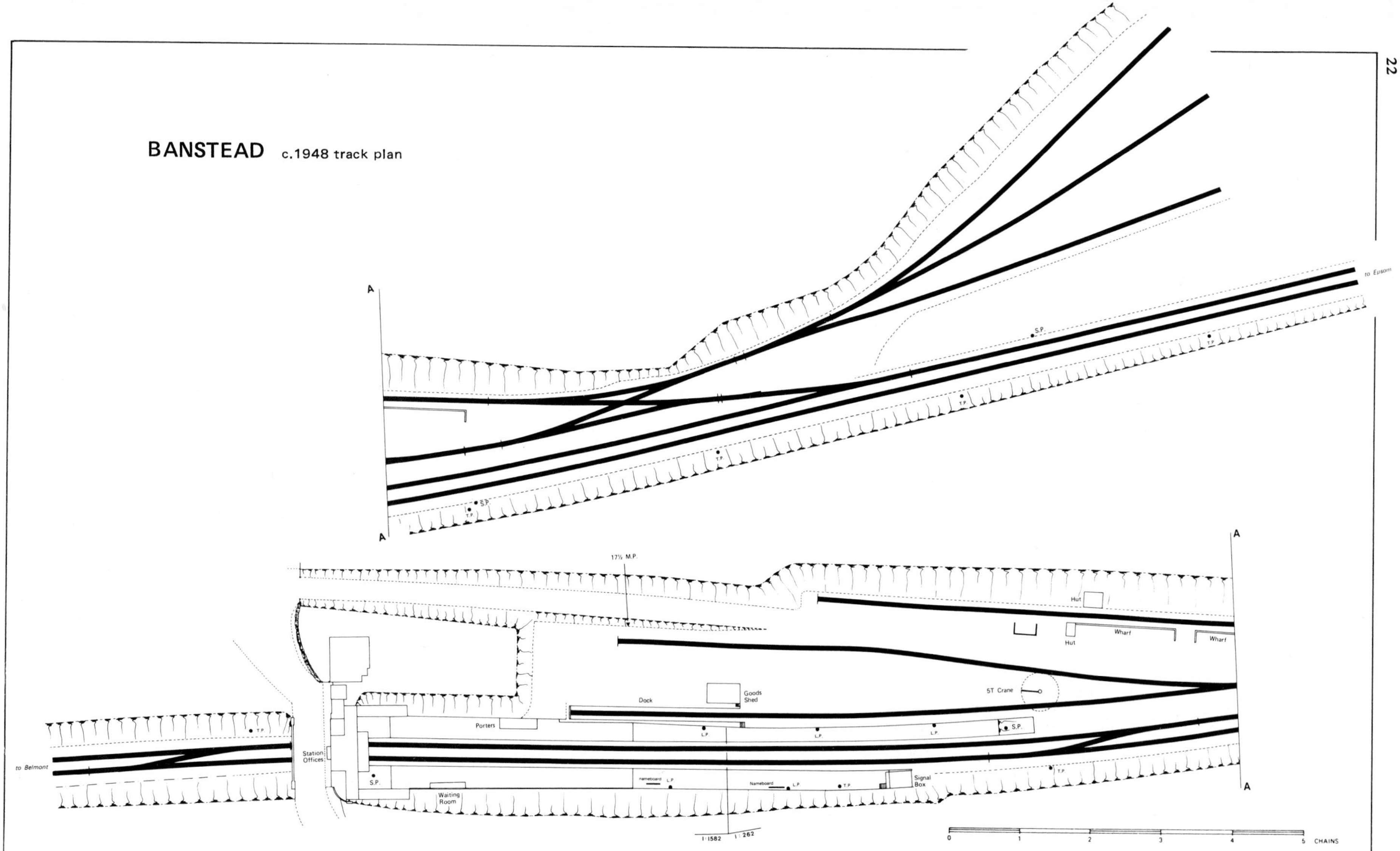

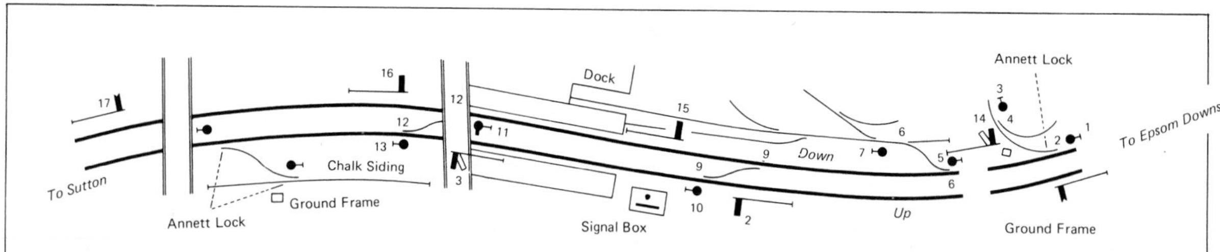

to Epsom

S.P.

17¼ M.P.

A

A

Wharf

Wharf

Hut

Hut

5T Crane

S.P.

Goods Shed

Dock

Signal Box

Porters

Waiting Room

Station Offices

S.P.

to Belmont

1:262

1:1582

CHAINS

0 1 2 3 4 5

c.1900 signalling diagram

Annett Lock

To Epsom Downs

Ground Frame

Up

Down

Dock

Signal Box

Chalk Siding

Ground Frame

Annett Lock

To Sutton

'Closely Observed Trains' at Banstead in the 1920s.

H. F. Wheeller

0—6—2T No. 2169 in Banstead yard on 23rd April 1935. The passenger train is a 'down' electric with ex-LBSC main line 'thirds' serving as trailers between each three-coach motor set. Early goods traffic was sparse as there was little industry on the branch, although coal was carried for domestic use and for the various hospitals and schools. After 1920 home building increased, the urban sprawl of London encircling Banstead Village. In the period 1925-38 a regular goods train (of varying length) was run, as the photographs show.   *H. F. Wheeller*

The Saxby and Farmer box at Banstead (*above*) on 14th April 1968 and (*left*) in 1950. It closed, along with the box at Belmont, on 21st December 1969, the yard itself having closed some years before, on 7th September 1964.   *J. Scrace and D. Clayton*

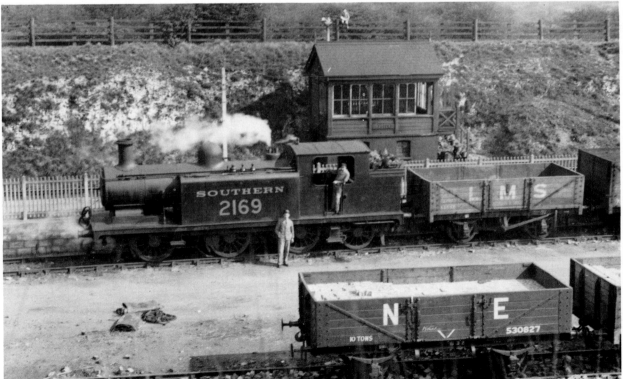

No. 2169 and crew again, on 23rd April 1935.

H. F. Wheeller

Banstead yard on 6th June 1953. The staff occupied spare moments with gardening and, as well as tending the usual array of shrubs and flowers, cut the station name in the chalk embankment. *G. Hookham*

Mogul No. 31832 shunting the small yard on 5th July 1964. At first no freight facilities were provided at all at Banstead, odd consignments and parcels, etc. being loaded at the platform. The sidings were laid out from about 1880, those by the station being principally for coal. Further along the layout included 'Crockett's siding', like the 'chalk siding' controlled by groundframe and Annett's Key. From the mid 'sixties the yard served as a fuel oil distribution point, GULF road tankers filling up from bogie tanks stabled on the centre road.

J. Spencer Gilks

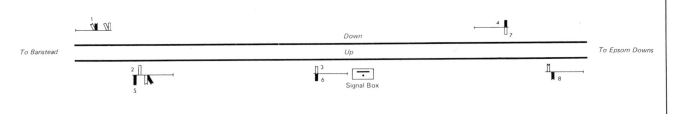

'C' INTERMEDIATE c.1900 signalling diagram

To Banstead

Down

Up

To Epsom Downs

Signal Box

'C' intermediate, 800 or so yards from Banstead cabin, with the precarious siting typical of these boxes. Relief signalman R. S. Graves stands vigil on 7th June 1928. *The late E. Wallis*

The up home and down starting signal controlled from 'C' intermediate (distant background) on 7th June 1928 together with down distant (equipped with Coligny-Welch lamp and spectacles for year-round use), operated from Epsom Downs box. Early indication of Southern ownership is the concrete fencing, supplied from the new works at Exmouth Junction opened in 1925. *The late E. Wallis*

28

Derby Day, 1877, and fifteen locomotives await the return trip to Sutton and beyond. The original of this well-known photograph for many years hung in the station master's office at Epsom Downs. A turntable was necessary for raceday traffic and a few wagons of coal were taken down for refuelling on the eve of such occasions. At first a small two-road wooden engine shed was provided but the paucity of traffic in the long periods between race meetings made it redundant for much of the time. It was removed after only a few years, leaving the coal stage, turntable and water tank. The fifteen locomotives visible were all of Craven design, the most notable and appropriate occupying the foreground, No. 40 *Epsom* as rebuilt by Mr. Stroudley.

Collection of the late E. Wallis

EPSOM DOWNS

Although the Derby, as a national event, had been reported in decline throughout the nineteenth century, and receipts were invariably disappointing, a 'raceday' remained an impressive occasion, with marquees, stalls, etc. Considerable traffic had accrued through school outings, and at weekends throughout the summer swings, etc. were provided for children's amusement. The station buffet accordingly enjoyed considerable patronage.

Photos: Collection D. Wallis

Facilities afforded to royalty attending the Derby were on a more lavish scale. This was the tent erected for the refreshment of Queen Alexandra around 1910.
Collection D. Wallis

Derby specials await departure in 1907. The engine spurs were a later feature, being added in the years before 1904. The Royal Train waits on the extreme left, behind the usual decorated 4—4—2T. The usual branch train plying for trade on an ordinary weekday appeared incongruous, if not absolutely lost! The 'double diamond' code boards denote special trains. *Collection E. A. Course*

'Boys Brigade' recruits and younger contemporaries enjoy a Sunday 'on the Downs' around 1910 (*right*). Swings etc. were erected to occupy the younger visitors (*below*). *Collection D. Wallis*

Some of the multitude of staff drafted in for race meetings, the culmination being the Royal visit. As well as additional signalmen, extra porters, railway police and inspectors descended upon Epsom Downs on such days. Everyday trains terminated at Banstead whilst for days prior to the meeting LBSC offices in central London remained open after normal hours, catering for extra business.   *D. J. W. Brough*

It was considered a great honour to be involved in the working of the Royal Train and a number of views, more in the manner of 'souvenir' pictures for the staff, have survived. Special uniforms were issued by the LBSCR, shown to particular advantage (*right*), with No. 78 on 2nd June 1911. No. 15 worked the 'Royal' in 1903 (*above*),   *Collection D. J. W. Brough and K. Nunn/LCGB*

Epsom Downs in 1950. An awning for the entrance was allowed for in the contractor's plans but never installed. The low central part of the building was the general waiting room, with ladies waiting room to the left. For many years, of course, this was strictly segregated into 1st and 2nd class. On the far left were the toilets, lamp room and a lobby for porters and enginemen. The station master's residence formed the rest of the building, with four bedrooms, and living room at the front. Behind the station master had his office, next to the ticket office proper.

D. Clayton

The Epsom Races, being a great English institution, were naturally plagued by evil weather, the great British brolly coming into its own. The pleasure seekers hurrying to get out of the wet (*left*) had a choice of ticket office on such busy days, dependent on destination, etc., a device to ease congestion and delay. The platform view (*top*) allows a glimpse of the lengthy awning removed by BR (*see p. 38*). The view above requires no comment!

Collection R. C. Riley

34

For much of the year the terminus was under-used and almost empty, particularly in the middle of the day. This effect, if anything, is heightened by a two coach steam train, in June 1928.

Collection R. C. Riley

Race Day, 1926. The majesty of the pre-war years is beginning to fade to something more prosaic, but the scene is still one of bustle and activity. Although the Southern began transferring traffic to the more convenient Tattenham Corner almost immediately, the most grievous loss being the Royal Train, the decline was slow and prolonged. Many services remained and it was not until the mid-fifties that race trains were seriously reduced. Engines left to right are 'E5' 0—6—2T No. B587 on 'Race Special No. 4', and '13s' Nos. 84 and 26 on specials Nos. '6' and '3' respectively. Pullmans for special trains, some of which are seen here, spent the last war stored at Epsom Downs out of use and painted grey.

A. B. MacLeod

Epsom Downs was notable for its long-lived and fine array of signals. Numbers on the arms referred to individual platforms whilst smaller arms were also provided. Lettered 'C', they were 'calling on' signals which enabled trains to enter partly occupied platforms.

Collection J. Scrace and D. Clayton

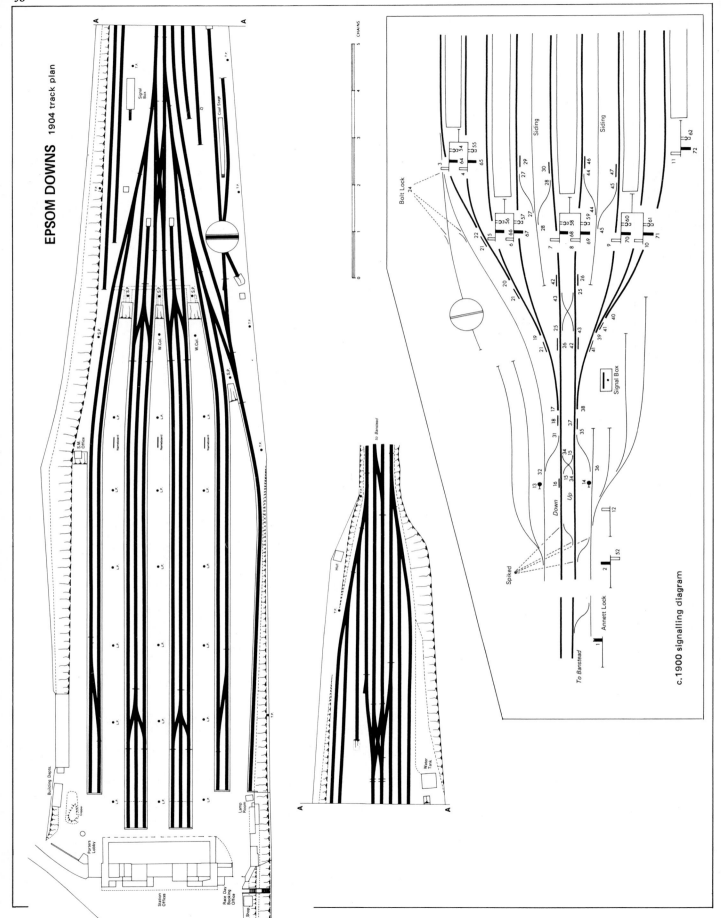

EPSOM DOWNS 1904 track plan

c.1900 signalling diagram

BR signals, in less flamboyant style, on 14th April
1968. *J. Scrace*

Epsom Downs box, 14th April 1968. The original
signal box dating from the opening of the line was
replaced by this much larger example in 1889. The
new box, most unusual in having a cladding of
corrugated iron, controlled, in addition to the
station area itself, a private siding serving the
Kensington and District School. Prior to the opening of the latter in 1880, the siding had been for
the use of a Mr. Gadsden of North Looe Farm and
was named accordingly. The following instructions
regulated its use:

'Epsom Downs: Gadsdens or North Looe Farm
Siding. This is on the UP side of the line,
between Epsom Downs and Banstead. The
points are fitted with Annett's Lock, the key of
which, when withdrawn from the frame, locks
the UP signals at Epsom Downs, and breaks the
signalling instrument circuit between Banstead
and Epsom Downs. The UP signals cannot be
lowered unless the Key is in the lock in the
Epsom Downs signal box, nor can the points
at the Siding be opened unless the Key is in the
lock attached to the points. The Station Master
at Epsom Downs must instruct the Driver and
Guard of the Goods Train appointed to do the
work at the Siding when to call, and send a
Porter to take and bring the Key back. Engines
must not be allowed into the Siding for a greater
distance than 36 yards from the Siding Gate.
All trucks for this Siding must be invoiced to
Epsom Downs Station and properly labelled.'

The interior view shows Mr. Hall on duty in his
box in July 1973. The chevroned levers applied
detonators automatically, those pointing down
indicating the 'down' line and vice-versa. The box
burned down on 16th November 1981 and for a
time the line was singled and worked as a shuttle
service only. Through services were restored on 3rd
October 1982 and full colour light signalling (controlled from the new Clapham Junction box)
inaugurated. Sutton signal box closed at the same
time. *Photos: J. Scrace and N. W. Hearn*

The station on 24th May 1972. There was an awning, running the width of the building on this side, removed by BR in the early 1950s. The removal of the runround loops mark the decline of the Derby traffic, the lavish electric service having also suffered curtailment. There had still been up to six trains an hour each way in the early 1950s, direct to London Bridge and Victoria, but by 1958 off-peak trains were running only half-hourly. Further reductions followed, particularly in the through service, and the Sunday trains, resurrected on electrification, were again withdrawn in May 1969. By 1958 the great majority of race specials worked to Tattenham Corner and subsequently the only provision for extra traffic was to increase the length of ordinary trains on Derby Day. Not long after this photograph was taken, the tracks at Epsom Downs were reduced to two only.   *D. Thompson*

Electric stock at the terminus on 8th March 1869. The Southern Railway extended the third rail system to Epsom Downs initially via West Croydon, and electric trains operated from London Bridge to Epsom Downs on 17th June 1928. A 20-minute service was operated in morning and evening rush hours and Saturday mornings; at other times and on Sundays, a 30-minute service was provided. In the rush hours trains ran all stations Epsom Downs to Norwood Junction and then non-stop to London Bridge. When the 30-minute service was in operation, trains ran all stations to London Bridge except Honor Oak Park and Brockley. On Sundays, they stopped at all stations Epsom Downs to London Bridge. The headcode carried was 'O'.

At this time the Victoria trains to Sutton continued as on the A.C. schedules, i.e. a 20-minute service in the rush hours via West Croydon to Sutton only. In the early '30s these trains were extended to Epsom Downs. This meant a service of six trains an hour on the branch in rush hours and four trains at other times. D.C. electric trains consisted of 3-coach motor sets and one of these was used in slack times. In the rush hours the 3-coach sets were used with a pair of trailers between them, making 8-coach trains. Victoria trains carried the headcode '5'.

A. A. Jackson

4–4–2T No. B21 near Belmont in June 1933 on a Pullman Race Special. Cars included *Alberton* (a 'Southern Belle' 1st Brake), *Princess Patricia* and *Pavilion*.
Dr. I. C. Allen

LOCOMOTIVES AND OPERATIONAL NOTES

Race traffic was the *raison d'être* of the Epsom Downs branch and remained so for many decades. The area served, with its thin chalk soils, was not ideal for farming and there were only a few small villages dotted around, so traffic was very light when no race meetings were being held. Sunday services were very soon withdrawn and not restored on a schedule until electrification. Several through trains were nevertheless operated, for visitors to the local hospitals. These terminated at Banstead and were parked on the main line between Banstead and Epsom Downs on both 'up' and 'down' lines. The trains worked back to London later in the afternoon.

Race day traffic was very heavy and the loco department was under considerable strain finding power for all the trains. Tender engines were used in the early days when a turntable, as well as an engine shed, was provided. 'A' class 0–6–0Ts, the 'Terriers' (or 'Rooters') arrived at West Croydon shed in the 1890s and, with sets of old four-wheelers, were used on the branch until motor train working began, on 11th June 1906. 'D1' 0–4–2Ts, Nos. 605 and 627 were sent to West Croydon in 1909 for these motor workings and the number of these engines subsequently increased steadily. The 'D1s' could operate two coaches and so they gradually replaced 'Terriers'

in the London area. The last 'Terriers' worked from Coulsdon shed as the Crystal Palace motors and the last 'Terrier' at West Croydon was No. 661, transferred to Littlehampton in August 1920. Various 'D1' class engines were shedded at West Croydon and in the period 1925-1928 the following engines were used on the Epsom Downs branch: 215, 220, 226, 259, 260, 269, 270, 282,

0–6–2T No. 2498 in Belmont yard, inevitably on a domestic coal working, 11th October 1935.
H. F. Wheeller

Southern Railway 0—6—2T No. 2404 at Sutton. These ex-Brighton tanks were useful for all manner of shunting, pilot and short haul goods work, and were often turned out for the branch goods.   *Lens of Sutton*

290, 296, 605, 615, 625, 627 and probably others, some only for short periods.

The engine was always hauling the train. If the motor set had arrived at Epsom Downs with the engine leading, it ran round the motor set and the 6-wheeled coaches were added at the rear. One 'down' train was the 4.36 ex-London Bridge, arriving at Epsom Downs at 5.36. The motor service was approximately one every ten minutes in the rush hours, but a large number terminated at Banstead, giving an approximately hourly service to Epsom Downs. The last train from Sutton to Epsom Downs was the 7.03 p.m., but the service to Banstead con-

tinued till 10.30. Extra trains ran on Wednesdays and Saturdays, at 11.38 and 12.20 p.m. There were also a few through motor trains to or from Wimbledon via Mitcham Junction. One was the 11.46 a.m. from Epsom Downs. A 'down' train was the 7.39 from Wimbledon to Banstead arriving at 8.07 p.m. An extra train from Sutton on Saturdays only, the 2.07 p.m., always consisted of a motor set, hauled by a non-motor fitted engine, often a 'D3' 0—4—4T.

Branch goods trains were worked by various 'E1' class 0—6—0Ts in LBSC days and possibly other types. In Southern days various 0—6—2Ts of classes 'E3', 'E4', 'E4X', 'E6' and 'E6X' were used, from West Croydon and later Norwood Junction shed. 'C2X' 0—6—0s and subsequently moguls were used on domestic coal workings as late as 1964. Oil was also a significant post-war item. Building supplies from the mid 'twenties, especially so following electrification in 1928, were also important. By the outbreak of war in 1939 a decade or more of housing development left the branch basically a London commuter line. Race days brought greater variety, with Marsh 4—4—2Ts powering the faster and more important turns, notably, of course, the Royal Train. Many types of engine were pressed into service, with a variety of stock. 'Spare' locos for emergency use were often stabled at Sutton on race-days, on the headshunt described on page 7. After 1923 even ex-LSW 'T9' 4—4—0s could be found on this duty.

In the period 1926-28, the regular rail motor shuttle service was entirely suspended from about 9.30 a.m. while

0—4—2T No. 290 at Sutton in SR days. The original motor trains started work on 11th June 1906 and consisted of a 'Terrier' 0—6—0T and one large open saloon coach. The train could be driven as usual from the engine, or could be controlled from a driving compartment at the opposite end of the coach, with the engine pushing. This service was run from West Croydon to Epsom Downs. Later a number of these trains terminated at Belmont and some ran from Sutton to Belmont only. As traffic slowly increased, it was found that the single coach was insufficient and so 'D1' class 0—4—2 tanks and coaches were used. At first these consisted of the engine in the middle of two driving trailers, but later the trains comprised engine, compartment, trailer, saloon and driving trailer. Various types of coach sets were in use, some compartment ones, and some compartment sets with corridors. In 1926-28 special services were run on Whitsun and August Bank Holidays and 4-coach motors were used, with the engine sandwiched between two 2-coach trailer sets.
                                                                                              H. F. Wheeller

A Victoria-Epsom Downs electric train passing through Banstead in 1938. It consists of a 3-car motor set, probably LSW type bodies, and a 2-car trailer set. These latter coaches, 'swingers', were ex-LBSC main line thirds and would have been followed by a further three coach motor set, making a total of eight vehicles. *G. Hookham*

0—6—2T No. 2472 in an off-peak moment with a motley collection of vehicles. *H. F. Wheeller*

the race traffic was run, and local services were only resumed in the late afternoon. Race trains had by this time been provided with bogie stock of various kinds. The all-first class train was often composed of the ex-LBSC 'City Limited' coaches hauled by an 'I3' 4—4—2T. On at least one occasion this train was hauled by an ex-SECR 'H' class 0—4—4T piloted by an ex-LBSC 'E5' 0—6—2T. The Pullman specials were also similarly 4—4—2T hauled.

One of the many workings of interest arising from the line's racecourse connections were the special horse-box trains, covered by Norwood Junction shed. On 3rd August 1959 'E3' 0—6—2T No. 582 was on duty and began by working light engine to Eardley for shunting 5.58 a.m. to 12.17 p.m. The loco then returned to Norwood shed, arriving at 12.46, leaving 'light' for Epsom Downs at 6.25 p.m., arriving 6.54. It was then ready to work the 7.33 p.m. horse-box train to London Bridge. The empty boxes were timed to arrive at New Cross Gate at 9.03 that

evening. It was for police horses, not race-horses, the mounted policemen travelling out on the Bank Holiday Saturday and returning on the Monday evening.

The Epsom Downs commuter trains ran to London Bridge and Victoria, but race trains sometimes had a more varied origin. Pullman expresses before the war ran from Victoria via the Mitcham Junction route to Sutton, reaching the terminus in 31 minutes. Following the Grouping, the Royal Train, remaining steam-hauled, used Tattenham Corner instead of Epsom Downs. In steam days, trains from the coast divided at Sutton, one portion for London Bridge, the other for Victoria and one train in the morning was slipped. This portion usually comprised two coaches, although sometimes a six-wheeled slip van sufficed. After the London Bridge portion had cleared the station, a tank engine, 'D1' 0—4—2T, 'E4' or 'E5' 0—6—2T or an 'I2' 4—4—2T with two coaches, backed on and took the combined train to Victoria.

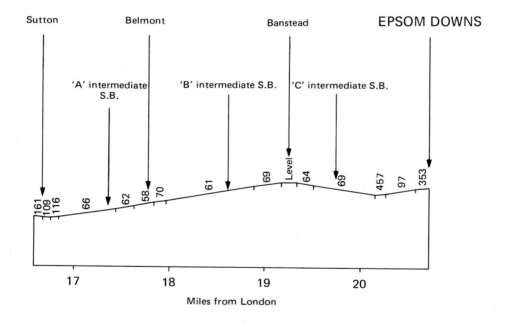

Station Approach, Sutton.

An old postcard view of Sutton station c.1905.

E. Crawforth

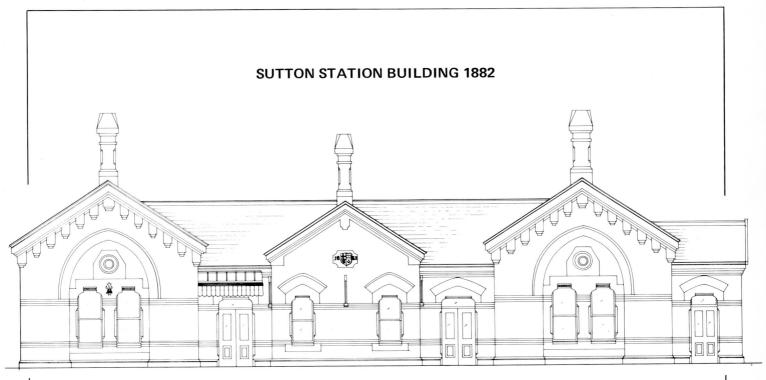

SUTTON STATION BUILDING 1882

SCALE — 2mm to 1 foot

BELMONT STATION BUILDING

S O U T H   E N D   E L E V A T I O N

N O R T H   E N D
E L E V A T I O N

F O R E C O U R T   E L E V A T I O N

BELMONT FOOTBRIDGE

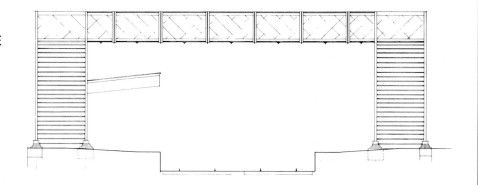

SCALE — 2 mm to 1 foot

BANSTEAD STATION BUILDING 1938

E L E V A T I O N   T O   R O A D

P L A N

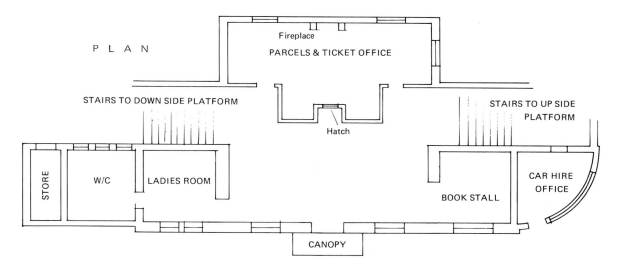

Fireplace

PARCELS & TICKET OFFICE

Hatch

STAIRS TO DOWN SIDE PLATFORM

STAIRS TO UP SIDE PLATFORM

STORE

W/C

LADIES ROOM

BOOK STALL

CAR HIRE OFFICE

CANOPY

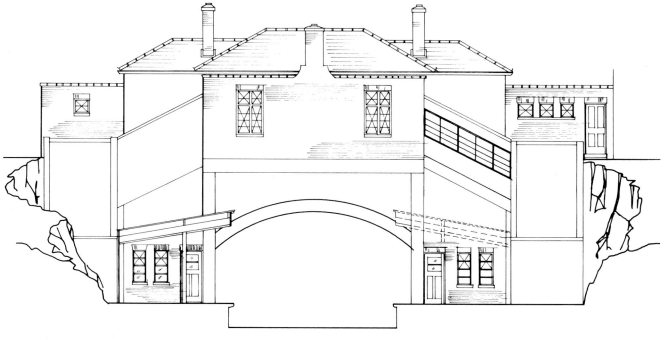

E L E V A T I O N   T O   R A I L S

SCALE — 2 mm to 1 foot

E L E V A T I O N   T O   P L A T F O R M

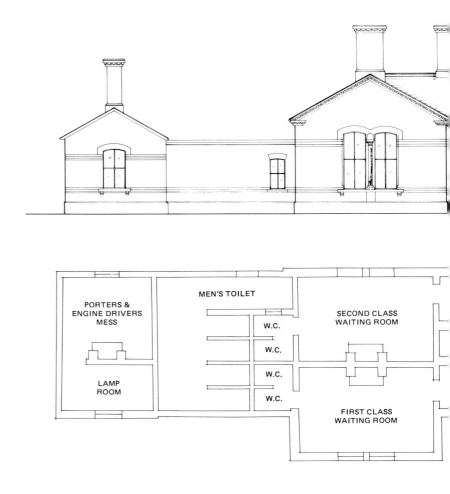

PORTERS & ENGINE DRIVERS MESS	MEN'S TOILET		SECOND CLASS WAITING ROOM
	W.C.		
	W.C.		
	W.C.		
LAMP ROOM	W.C.		FIRST CLASS WAITING ROOM

SCALE — 2 mm to 1 foot

EPSOM DOWNS STATION BUILDING

F O R E C O U R T   E L E V A T I O N

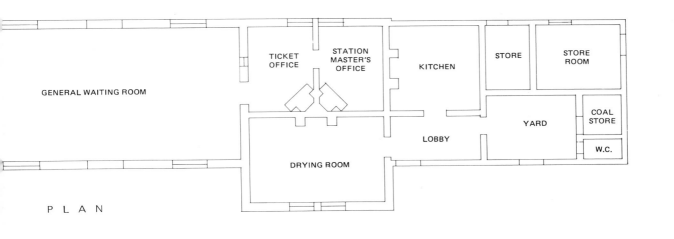

GENERAL WAITING ROOM

TICKET OFFICE

STATION MASTER'S OFFICE

KITCHEN

STORE

STORE ROOM

DRYING ROOM

LOBBY

YARD

COAL STORE

W.C.

P L A N

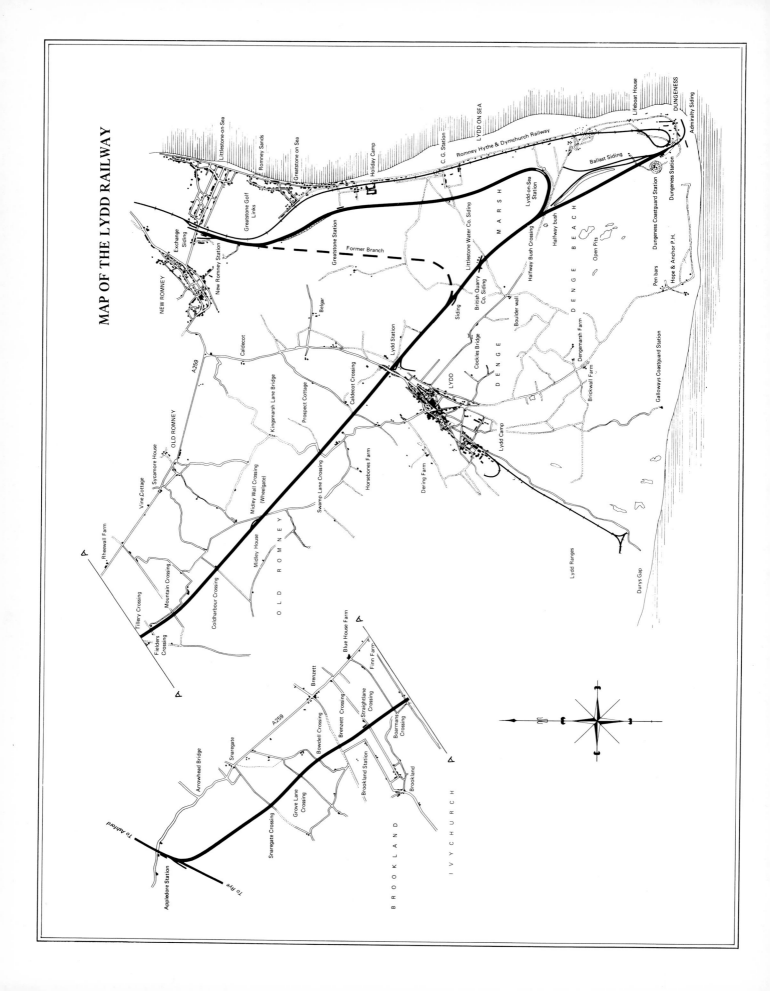

MAP OF THE LYDD RAILWAY

The Lydd Railway
The New Romney and Dungeness Branches

THE Lydd Railway developed under the aegis of the SER and was built with high but unrealized hopes of developing a thriving cross-Channel steamer traffic. In addition, the Board of the SER firmly predicted that the shingle traffic (extensively used in the building and pottery trades) would grow and become to the South Eastern what coal was to other lines serving industrial areas.

The foreland at Dungeness is a peculiar feature from a geographical point of view and the offshore currents contrive to deposit a limitless supply of shingle; indeed much of the area crossed by the new railway was, until relatively recently, former sea water displaced by the ever growing foreland. Quite how the nation's building firms would have coped with several extra million tons a year of this unattractive material was never put to the test. Needless to say, the expectations for its sale were never realized if for no other reason than supplies were readily available from sites much nearer to London and similar metropolitan centres.

To make matters worse for the unfortunate SER, the proposed port was also destined never to appear and the line which ran from Appledore to Lydd, there splitting to New Romney and Dungeness, was never exactly overtaxed. The area was flat, sparsely populated and its exposed nature could make it as bleak and unfriendly as any Pennine fell.

As long ago as 1866, a scheme had surfaced for a branch off the SER's Ashford to Hastings line, from Appledore to New Romney and Dungeness. This was the erstwhile New Romney Railway, abandoned in 1870 before any kind of building work had been embarked upon. The lucrative possibilities involved in the development of port facilities at Dungeness had been eyed by various persons of entrepreneurial bent for some time and it was not long before specific proposals arose once more. These notions were drawn together in the Rye and Dungeness Railway and Pier Act, authorized by Parliament on 5th August 1873 and, although the powers therein were not made use of, the SER was careful to have them transferred to itself two years later.

Schemes with Dungeness as a new steamer terminal continued throughout the 1870s. Evidently Sir Edward Watkin, Chairman of the SER, was an enthusiastic supporter of all this, encouraged by the possibility of finance coming largely from the public purse. A new, shorter route between London and Paris was the goal and the new service would operate the sixty miles between Dungeness and Le Treport, a fishing and holiday town having rail links with Paris, a hundred and fourteen miles away. If Dungeness could be similarly linked with London, involving a distance of about seventy miles, a new route between the two capitals, shorter than any existing, would be created.

The first stage of this grandiose scheme once again involved a new line from Appledore. Further Parliamentary work was necessary and the SER was eventually successful when its Lydd Railway Act was approved on 8th April

Stirling 'A' class 4—4—0 running round at Dungeness in the days when tender engines regularly worked the line. It appears, from photographs at least, that engines worked tender first on the 'down' run, a journey which in winter must have been singularly unpleasant. 'D3' 0—4—4Ts and 'H' class 0—4—4Ts, used quite regularly on the branch and fitted with storm sheets, were described with commendable understatement as 'only a little less trying'. *Collection A. M. Riley*

1881. The new line, nominally independent, presented no engineering difficulties and was worked from the first by the SER, who took it into official ownership in 1895.

The flat terrain meant that construction proceeded rapidly and indeed it had begun before the Act was formally authorized, being complete as far as Lydd before the end of the year. Appledore to Lydd was opened for all traffic on Wednesday, 7th December 1881, with the Dungeness section opening for freight only at the same time. Passenger services on this section eventually began on 1st April 1883. The portion of the branch from Lydd to New Romney had been authorized on 24th July 1882 and opened on 19th June 1884. Powers had also been obtained to reduce the distance to Ashford in readiness for the rise of the new steamer port. In 1882 powers were obtained to construct a line from Appledore to Headcorn on the Tonbridge-Ashford main line, via Tenterden, increased in the next year to include an extension northwards to Maidstone. None of this ever materialized and Appledore remained over seventy miles from London.

The SER was particularly attracted by an idea which seemed to combine neatly two activities which were to make the line's fortune. The company had bought 1,000 acres of land at Dungeness for only £5 an acre and, as the shingle was extracted for shipment to an eagerly awaiting nation, the resulting holes would be ideal for the intended new dock. Needless to say, this was all too good to be true, and a few pits are now the only evidence that remains of the SER's forlorn expectations.

The shingle extracted did find a use as ballast over most of the company's system, but virtually the only traffic that really developed on the branch was military. The great expanse of the Marsh was ideal for testing high explosives (one type was even christened 'Lyddite') and there was an extensive army camp at Lydd. Some four or five miles of standard gauge line, owned by the War Department and serving the various works, connected with the company's line at Lydd.

The branch came to be extraordinary in two respects. The Southern extensively re-aligned it in 1937 and it also connected with a 15 inch gauge line, the Romney, Hythe and Dymchurch Railway, opened from Hythe to New Romney in 1927 and extended to Dungeness two years later.

The SR's re-alignment was carried out under the Southern Railway Act of 1935 and was brought into use on 4th July 1937. The junction of the New Romney and Dungeness sections was moved nearer to Dungeness and a new line built northward to rejoin the original line just south of New Romney. Two extra halts were opened, Lydd on Sea and Greatstone on Sea, and 'Lydd' was renamed 'Lydd Town'. The Dungeness section was closed to passengers at the same time, on the tenuous basis that the new Lydd on Sea halt would provide alternative facilities, despite being over a mile away. The resited line was intended to tap the growing traffic from holiday camps which were planned in the vicinity.

Despite some growth in these camps, traffic continued to decline and by the early 'sixties even on summer days trains rarely contained more than a handful of passengers. Dungeness had closed completely by May 1963 and the New Romney services ceased on 6th March 1967. Passenger services were withdrawn from the rest of the branch at the same time but the odd train load of shingle is still taken from a site near to Dungeness, and special trains also still run in association with the nearby nuclear power station opened in 1965.

A 'B' class 4—4—0, its bulk and power at odds with the surroundings, awaits departure from the isolated Dungeness terminus. Having traversed the Marsh tender first, the crew were doubtless anticipating a somewhat less windblown return. *Lens of Sutton*

Stroudley 0—4—2 No. B184 runs into Appledore on a 'down'
Ashford-Hastings stopping train on 17th October 1929. 'Staggered'
platforms were fairly common practice on the SER and crossing was
a procedure requiring care and alertness on the part of the passenger.
An insight into the branch train procedures can be had from a
detailed report on an incident at Appledore in the *Railway Engineer*
of July 1899:

*Appledore, S.E.R., on the 26th December. Lieut.-Col. H. A.
Yorke, R.E. reports:—*

That a horse-box, which was to be attached to the 10.45 a.m.
train from Ashford to Hastings, was propelled by a 4-coupled
tender engine against the train with such violence that eight
passengers were badly hurt, two of them having their legs broken,
and much damage done to the rolling stock. The train consisted
of engine, tender, and 5 coaches fitted with the automatic vacuum
brake, the blocks being on the wheels at the time of the collision.

There are two lines through Appledore Station, the approxi-
mate direction of which is north-east and south-west, and there
are up and down platforms. The platforms are not opposite to
each other, the southern end of the up-platform being opposite
to the northern end of the down platform, an arrangement
which was not uncommon in former days. At the southern end
of the station there is a double junction between the main lines
and the single line branch to Lydd and New Romney, with
facing points on the down line. About the centre of the station
there is a trailing siding connection with each of the main lines,
and north of the place there is a cross-over road between the up
and down lines, between which and the station, there is a public
road level-crossing.

The branch train from New Romney, due at Appledore at
10.52 a.m., arrived there on the up line at 11.3 a.m., being 11
minutes late. The front vehicle on it was a horse-box, which
was to be forwarded to Rye with the down train for Hastings,
due to leave Appledore at 11 a.m. When the branch train ran
into the station the stationmaster and shunter were on the up
platform awaiting its arrival, and the down train was standing
alongside the down platform. As soon as the branch train stopped
the guard called out to the stationmaster and shunter that there
was a horse-box for Rye. The shunter at once uncoupled the
horse-box, engine, and tender from the train and gave a hand-
signal to driver Whitewood to go forward over the points of the
cross-over road, but no-one informed him what was to be done
with the horse-box. It is usual for the engines of the branch
trains to be uncoupled immediately after their arrival at this
place, and to get across on to the down line for the purpose of
running round their trains, which are then drawn out on to the
branch and backed to the down platform ready for the return

journey to New Romney. The branch train to which reference is
made in this report is, as stated, due at 10.52, and the Hastings
train is due at 11, and it generally happens that the engine of the
branch train is allowed to run round before the arrival of the
other train. Driver Whitewood went forward over the points as
directed, and immediately afterwards he received a hand-signal
from the shunter to come back through the cross-over road on to
the down line.

There is no doubt that Whitewood did not know what the
intention was as regards the horse-box, and thought that he had
to run round his train as usual, and that the horse-box was to be
left in the up sidings. He therefore reversed his engine and
opened the regulator, and came back at a fast speed so as to get
round his train, which was then due to start on its return journey,
as quickly as possible. As he was approaching the down platform
he saw the stationmaster making signals to him to stop. He says
that he had already shut off steam, and he at once applied his
brake and reversed his engine; but before the speed was materially
reduced the horse-box collided with the rear van of the down
train, which was still standing at the down platform. Both driver
Whitewood and his fireman were thrown down and hurt; several
passengers in the train received very serious injuries, and the
damage to the rolling stock was considerable. Whitewood esti-
mates the speed at which his engine was moving at 7 m. an h.,
but judging from the effects of the collision, it was probably
considerably higher.

Both Whitewood and Whibley were exceedingly careless.
Although, therefore, these men, who had been on duty about
6 h. 40 min., were not told, as they should have been, what was
going to be done with the horse-box, there is no excuse for their
negligence, Whitewood is more culpable.

But while thus condemning the conduct of these men, it
must be admitted that they are not the only ones in fault. Both
the stationmaster and the shunter seem to have assumed that the
driver knew what he had to do, and neither of them took the
trouble to inform him as to the destination of the horse-box.
Had either of them done so, the collision would not have
occurred. The shunter on this occasion was working under the
direct superintendence of the stationmaster, and may be absolved.
But the stationmaster evidently failed in his duty in this respect,
and must therefore share in the responsibility for the accident.

In later years, to avoid blocking the main line whilst engines for
the branch ran round their train, the goods yard would be used in a
series of manoeuvres. A study of the branch diagram will reveal a
run round facility allowing arrivals from the branch to back into the
yard, run round the train, and then shunt back over to the down
platform to await passengers for New Romney, etc. *H. C. Casserley*

The 'up' platform at Appledore, 25th April 1947. By this time the wooden shunting signal had been replaced by an upper quadrant rail-built example. The stub siding was mainly used by permanent way gangs, their trolleys parked there when not in use. It was removed in the early 1960s. There was a small wooden structure below the bracket signal by the level crossing. It originally sheltered the porters in moments of rest, before they were removed to even smaller premises, on the far side of the crossing and remote from the station.

H. C. Casserley

APPLEDORE

Little has changed at Appledore since the opening of the station on 13th February 1851. Beyond the level crossing gates is the former gatekeeper's house.
J. Scrace

The station retained most of its original features and the various additions of the years are clearly discerned. The plain brick wall at the far end of the building masked a gents' toilet added in 1860, whilst the central, original, part of the building dates from 1851. Through the platform entrance was the booking hall with a ladies waiting room off to the left. The ticket office also stood to the left, whilst the small extension in the foreground was originally the station master's office. Drastic alterations were envisaged in 1934, when proposals to alter the building appeared. The station master's office would have become part of a 'combined signal cabin and booking office'. The station master would have been evicted to a smaller room overlooking the platform, formed from part of the old booking office. The authorities eventually decided against such an upheaval and the proposal was abandoned.
G. Reeve

Signal sighting was difficult at Appledore due to the intrusive canopy. To overcome the problem, the starter was mounted on a bracket, originally an SER lattice, later replaced by a Southern rail-built structure. This modern Southern Region box opened at Appledore around 1957, attention having been given to the old box in October 1945, a 'proposed extension to the landing'. The four BR gates replaced an earlier set of four, of SECR origin.
J. Scrace

54

The canopy on the 'up' side at Appledore was a later addition, being approved in the 1860s.
R. T. H. Platt

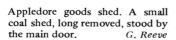

Appledore goods shed. A small coal shed, long removed, stood by the main door. *G. Reeve*

Wainwright 'H' class 0—4—4T No. 31329 at Appledore on Saturday, 28th June 1952 with the 6.28 p.m. from Ashford to Rye and New Romney. The two rear coaches comprised the latter portion, forming a push and pull set. Although No. 31329 carries a St. Leonards shed duty number, most workings were operated from Ashford shed.
R. F. Roberts

Evening at Appledore in 1951. The branch swung off to the left in the distance, the junction being brought slightly closer to the station during minor rearrangements in the 1900s. The moderately extensive goods yard handled the branch traffic as well as produce from surrounding farms, incoming coal, etc. Livestock was once important and special instructions were issued for their handling, viz: 'Cattle Train Arrangements Ashford Cattle Market — Tuesdays — Cattle from New Romney and Lydd for Ashford Market must be worked by the 6.28 a.m. Passenger Train ex-New Romney'.

'Appledore and New Romney Traffic, inclusive — Appledore Traffic to be loaded from Ashford by 4.05 p.m. Passenger Train whenever possible, failing this to be attached with other Branch Traffic by the 6.13 p.m. Passenger Train. Not more than 2 vehicles per Train must be attached.' The signal box is the original SER building. *L & GRP, courtesy David & Charles*

The 'down' side at Appledore in earlier days. This original signal had a low spectacle plate, thought to have been yet another attempt to overcome sighting difficulties. The view from a train about to reverse into the yard would have been obscured by the goods shed canopies. The 'down' platform canopy was in its turn remodelled. *Collection R. C. Riley*

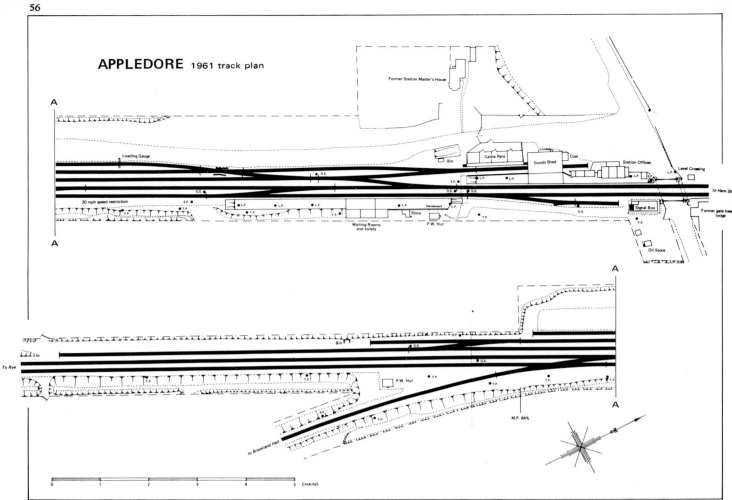

APPLEDORE 1961 track plan

Former Station Master's House

Loading Gauge

Cattle Pens

Goods Shed

Coal

Station Offices

Bin

G.S.

S.P.

L.P.

L.P.

Level Crossing

L.P.

G.S.

to Ham Street

20 mph speed restriction

S.P.

L.P.

L.P.

L.P.

T.P.

L.P.

Store

Nameboard

L.P.

Signal Box

T.P.

T.P.

T.P.

G.S.

Waiting Rooms
and toilets

P.W. Hut

T.P.

Oil Store

Former gate keeper's
lodge

A

To Rye

Bin

G.S.

G.S.

P.W. Hut

T.P.

T.P.

T.P.

T.P.

T.P.

T.P.

T.P.

M.P. 64¾

to Brookland Halt

0   1   2   3   4   5   CHAINS

Drewry petrol engine railcar entering the branch around 1933.

Dr. I. C. Allen

The more ancient, inland parts of 'the Marsh' near to Appledore station were converted into farmland of a sort by a complex system of drainage ditches. With such inauspicious labels as 'Cheyne Gut Sewer', the 'sewers' performed an identical role to that of the Fenland 'cuts' and indeed the two areas had many similarities. Windswept at the best of times, Brookland Halt stood on the Rye-New Romney road, some ¾ mile from the hamlet of Brookland. Understandably, traffic prospects were poor and this view taken prior to 1920 is the last we have of the station with passing loop intact.
Courtesy John Wimble

BROOKLAND

'The staff' at Brookland. This solitary gentleman was porter and ticket collector, and performed any other task as and when required. Although only a single member of staff attended the halt in later years, he did not cover the full operating period and his duties often fell to the train guard.   *Courtesy John Wimble*

New tank types available after Nationalization proved ideal for the area. LMS and BR 2—6—4Ts and 2—6—2Ts were designed with such turns in mind, stopping trains of several coaches over moderate distances interspersed with lightly loaded branch trains. No. 80034 was a regular engine in the early 'sixties, here at Brookland with a through service to London.
George Barlow

The line was relatively prosperous until after the Great War and in contrast to later cutbacks, consideration was given in the early years to various improvements. The first, around 1890, was for a horse dock, a short siding off the passing loop, at the north end of the station. The public road was to be extended past the station to serve the new dock. The proposal, referred to as 'the old scheme', was resurrected in enlarged form in 1899. In addition to the original 'horse dock siding' a cross-over was envisaged with a further siding, 'suitable for 12 trucks', taken past the station building on the north side, as far as the Rye-New Romney Road. The cost was estimated at £685. The trade outlook had altered for the worse by 1920, when further SECR plans, noting that none of the enlargements had been accomplished, now proposed a reduction in facilities.

Lens of Sutton

Elimination of the passing loop was the main feature of the 1920 measures, a useful method of boosting finances whilst disposing of redundant assets being to sell off the station building as a private dwelling. Conveyancing problems meant the SECR never saw the financial rewards of this particular stratagem. The Southern eventually concluded the sale, the station going 'as flats' in the 'thirties. A new footpath was taken along the track to a new building on the site of the old crossing keeper's hut illustrated on page 60.   *Lens of Sutton*

The waiting shed canopy, based on that at Appledore, was provided in 1915.

Lens of Sutton

In a more benign age, Wainwright 'H' class 0—4—4T No. 1305 departs for Lydd on 18th May 1936, leaving the unfortunate 'porter/signalman' to another lonely vigil.

H. C. Casserley

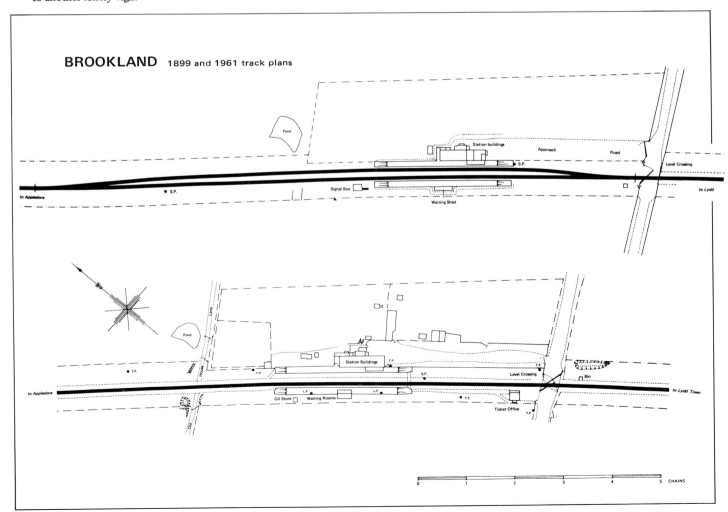

BROOKLAND 1899 and 1961 track plans

The ticket office, informal waiting room, etc. in BR guise and (naturally) deserted, on 19th September 1963. The *Kentish Express* of 5th November 1965, responding to closure threats, described the halt thus: 'its passengers have to walk across gravel to reach the platform which is bordered by tree-growing grass'.
D. Thompson

The English country branch. Ex-SECR 'C' class 0–6–0 No. 31218 with a single van drifts through Brookland in the early summer of 1960. Such scenes would utterly vanish before the decade was out.
T. Wright

Severe staff reductions were imposed along the line and in Southern days affairs were placed in the hands of the ubiquitous Grade One Porter. The varied duties of the Brookland stalwart have already been mentioned but in his absence the ensuing procedural complexity is an object lesson in the drawbacks of branch line operation in Britain. Crippled by regulations dating from the horse era, only a determination to simplify operation would have saved lines such as this for passenger traffic. The drama at Brookland illustrates the point: 'The Halt is staffed by one man. When Grade One Porter is booked off duty 'up' branch trains must stop at Home Signal. The Guard must then operate the Gates and lower signal to allow the train forward to the platform. The Guard must then replace Gates and Signal and collect tickets. Light Engines are prohibited when the Grade One Porter is off duty unless accompanied by a member of the Traffic Staff. The Guard must also light lamps when necessary. Last train of the day, lights to be put out by Guard. The keys for unlocking the cabin and gates are obtained from Lydd or Appledore stations and must be returned after use.'
H. C. Casserley

Midley Wall Crossing, one of fourteen on the line, circa 1930. Most of the crossings were gated and several were attended by full time keepers. Midley Wall, about two miles north of Lydd, was one of the most important. On the opening of the line, it had been described as a 'Passing Station', at first unused. 'Special Traffic Notice No. 102' issued by the SER in 1881 announced: 'There is an intermediate Signal Box between Brookland and Lydd Stations, and provided with a passing line, but will not be opened for Traffic at present. The Points will be bolted and locked for the Straight Line, and the Arms of the Signals taken out.' The extent to which such facilities were used, if at all, is not known.

Railway gatekeeping in this country became peculiarly the lot of women, odd in that conditions were exceptionally harsh (or not so odd perhaps). The buildings were of poor quality on the Lydd Railway (described as 'Shanty cottages' in the local press) and in all but three cases were not provided with gas, electricity or even water. No less than twelve ladies (and one man) faced redundancy in November 1965 when BR first announced its intention to close the line to passengers. A Mrs. Deirdre Dowling was the last incumbent at Midley Wall and must have faced a considerable task when first taking up the occupancy, already shabby in this 1930 photograph. A Mrs. Lena Deare, of Caldecot Crossing, near Lydd, delivered the most telling verdict. A widow, she was reported looking forward to closure, 'for the money and long hours it's not worth it.'
Collection John Wimble

MIDLEY WALL CROSSING

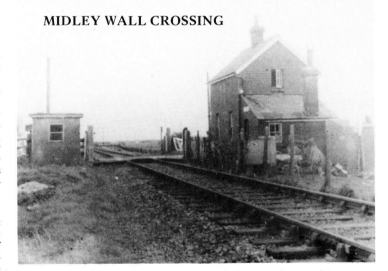

LYDD

c.1900 track plan

to Dungeness

S.P.

Disc signals

Loading Gauge

S.P.

Signal Box

Private Siding to ranges

Waiting Shed

Well

Tank House

S.P.

Station Buildings

Goods Shed

Cattle Pens

Advert Board

Disc signals

S.P.

to Appledore

1961 track plan

to New Romney & Dungeness

T.P.

T.P.

Disc signals

T.P.

S.P.

M.P. 71¾

T.P.

Signal Box

S.P.

Loading Gauge

L.P.

L.P.

L.P.

Nameboard

Oil Store

L.P.

Waiting Shed

Nameboard

L.P.

L.P.

Station Offices

Station Master's House

S.P.

W. Col.

Water Tower

Trolley Shed

Ground Frame

P.W. Hut

Coal Pens

Goods Shed

Cattle Pens

Level Crossing

1 in 100

1 in 260

Station

Road

to Brookland Halt

CHAINS

0 1 2 3 4 5

LYDD

Staff pose at Lydd in the early 1900s. Sighting difficulties again meant a bracket signal was necessary.   *Collection J. Scrace*

The War Office found the flat empty land south-east of Lydd ideal for gunnery ranges and a sizeable camp grew up, rivalling Lydd itself in size. A railway existed to carry troops and pieces from the camp the length of the test area to the coast, and at one time extended into the goods yard itself. It follows that troop traffic was often heavy, in this case with what appears to be members of the regimental band, about 1908. Troop traffic remained important, even into the late 1950s. The large detached house was the station master's residence.

Collection John Wimble

Lydd station and yard, circa 1900. The P.W. trolleys at this time were simply dumped by the lineside. *Lens of Sutton*

The only bridge taken across the branch was at Lydd. The volume of road traffic here was greater than at any other point, the SER deciding to erect a bridge in preference to the more usual crossing.
K. K. Koraitie

The line's solitary bridge, however, proved inadequate for the heavy traffic during the construction of Dungeness power station in 1961, and ironically a separate level crossing became necessary. The cost was £183, and whether the railway or the CEGB paid is not clear. *A. Schmilton*

A general rearrangement of the station was planned by the SER, proposals which, like so many connected with the line, were destined to be less than wholly fulfilled. A lengthy new waiting shed was planned at the country end of the 'up' platform (shown here in the 'sixties). This, together with an extension of the platform itself, was abandoned and the original station building was instead altered and enlarged. Small extensions appeared at each end, the one here, at the Appledore end, containing Ladies' and Gentlemen's toilets. At the far end, a further small addition contained lamp room and porters lobby and formed part of an enlarged ticket office and cloakroom. The whole was later taken over by the station master, for office space. The former cramped waiting room and booking office inside the building became a general waiting room and the former Ladies' toilet was converted to provide waiting accommodation for unsuspecting 1st class passengers.   *P. Tangye*

The wooden waiting shelter of 1910 in style so typical of the branch. The canopy was a much later feature, lacking the valancing used at Appledore and Brookland.   *P. Tangye*

66

Lydd in the mid-thirties. The signal cabin, of typical SER affinities, underwent certain minor alterations over the years. The steps originally led from the rear wall but following fire damage the cabin required complete recladding. The steps, along with a new toilet, appeared subsequently on the far side of the building. The old loco tender in the yard was the means by which drinking water reached the various stations, the crossing keeper's supply travelling in milk churns delivered by passenger train. In times of need the latter were served by the obliging Lydd P.W. gang, using one of their 'pump' trolleys.

Lens of Sutton

A cold clear December at Lydd, 1965. In 1938 the Southern considered installing a crane in the yard, yet another proposal which failed to materialize.
Alan A. Jackson

'C' class 0—6—0 No. 31218 pauses during shunting work at Lydd.
T. Wright

Class '2MT' No. 84028 leaves for New Romney on 10th June 1960. The versatile standard tanks eventually ousted the old SECR types in the last years of steam. Lydd had become 'Lydd Town' in 1937, distinguishing it from the new SR station at 'Lydd-on-Sea', one of two stations built on the new alignment.
T. Wright

The standard gauge Lydd Military Railway was built to connect Lydd Camp and its associated artillery test ranges with the new station at Lydd. Its principal purpose was the conveyance of the various materials required for such activities, including guns. The track, some six miles in length, was completed in 1883, but no locomotives were acquired until 1885, when two WD locos arrived from work on the erstwhile 'Suakin and Berber Railway' in the Sudan. Manning Wardle 0—6—0STs (WD Nos. 132 and 134), these pillars of Empire remained at work until 1906 and 1907 respectively, when they were replaced by 0—6—0T No. 2746 *Napier* (Hunslet Engine Co.) and No. 1882 *Nicholson*, an 0—4—2T built by Fowler & Co. These details come to us through excllent research published by O. J. Morris in *The Locomotive* of August 1934, the final two locos he notes being No. 4125 *Trafford*, a Manning Wardle 0—4—0ST acquired in 1916 and No. 4199 *Betty*, an Avonside engine of similar wheel arrangement acquired in 1917. The Great War was possibly the line's most active period but shortly after the Armistice the Royal Artillery Gunnery Establishment was closed, being replaced by a battalion of the Royal Tank Corps. Maintenance of the track had been neglected over the years and by the mid-twenties the cost of repairs, plus the continual expense of wayleave agreements, was not considered justified. The track was accordingly taken up in 1926/27 and the Lydd Military Railway came to an end.

(Top) A. E. Shaw, courtesy C. Turner
(Centre) Collection John Wimble

'Pump trolley' on the Lydd Military Railway, circa 1910. The family are probably related to a railway employee; this unconventional transport is thought to have been used for getting to the sea at Jury's Gap, a stretch of sandy beach between Dungeness and Camber.

Collection John Wimble

From Lydd the branch continued across the featureless Denge Marsh, to the terminus at Dungeness which initially handled goods traffic only. The straggling vegetation finally gave up some distance before Dungeness itself, leaving a strange, almost unreal landscape. The lack of human presence has always made the marsh ideal for wild life, particularly birds, and before the motor car students of ornithology made frequent use of the train. H. G. Alexander in *Seventy Years of Birdwatching* says: 'Dungeness beach itself is not so easily transformed by human ingenuity. Many years ago as I sat in the train that used to run from Lydd to the Dungeness lighthouse, a fellow traveller commented, as the train came over the first shingle banks: 'This is the last place God made, and he forgot to finish it' which really does give some idea of the strange nature of Dungeness beach.'

Shingle, with which the SER hoped to make the line's fortune, was garnered in monumental quantities over the years, to the present day, and various sidings were provided as the workings waxed and waned. The present British Quarrying Company siding, just north of the old Folkestone Water Company (formerly the Littlestone Water Company) pumping station, was sited between the 'old' and 'new' New Romney junctions. The vast and lonely workings only serve to enhance the brooding air of the marsh.

Working instructions for the sidings were typically complex; both were protected by ground frames unlocked by train staffs from Lydd signal box. Orders issued on the working of the siding stated that the Littlestone Water Company Siding was to be worked by the Ashford-Dungeness goods service and the British Quarrying Company Siding by 'a shunting engine'. Shunting orders were also issued — 'The wagons for this siding are propelled from Lydd, with a brake van, in which the guard must ride leading. The van must be propelled to the Dungeness side of the points leading into the siding and, after the hand brake has been fully applied on the van, detached and left on the single line whilst the siding is worked. After the work at the siding has been completed the brake van must be coupled to the rear of the train and the whole train hauled back to Lydd. The Company engine must not proceed into the siding beyond the boundary gate at which point ingoing and outgoing wagons must be exchanged, ingoing wagons being left immediately beyond the gate.'

G. Reeve

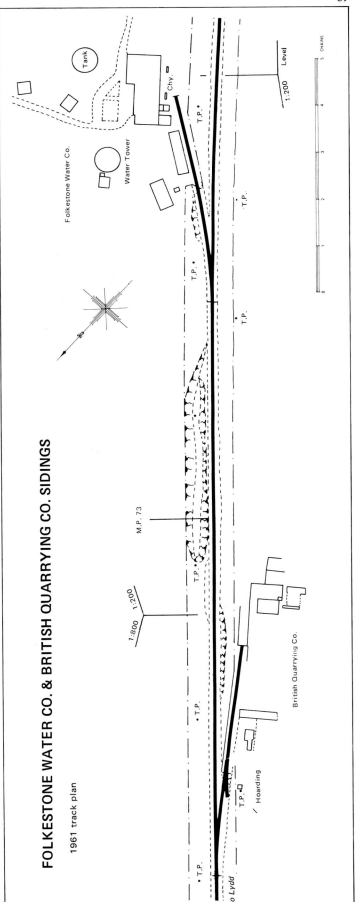

FOLKESTONE WATER CO. & BRITISH QUARRYING CO. SIDINGS

1961 track plan

The rudimentary terminus at Dungeness opened for passengers in April 1883, the New Romney section following just over a year later. The Dungeness portion was never afterwards much more than an adjunct and facilities remained primitive. Merely to reach Dungeness required determination and not a little patience on the part of the traveller. H. G. Alexander describes a visit to Dungeness in the early part of August 1905: 'We were staying at Rye for a few days, and we decided to go by train to Dungeness and spend the day there. This then meant taking the Ashford train from Rye to Appledore (the next station) and changing; then came the train down from Ashford, and when it had left Appledore a special train took passengers across the marsh to Lydd, where again we changed, to wait while our train went to New Romney and back; then it made its separate journey to Dungeness lighthouse! It sounds complicated and tedious, but apart from the necessity of climbing in and out of trains three times it was not as bad as it sounds. The trains were arranged to connect, and as far as I recall, the whole journey took little more than an hour. Even today, when there is a road from Lydd to Dungeness (there was none in 1905) the journey by car from Rye to Dungeness would normally take half an hour or more, with so many right-angle turns along the marsh roads.'

Lens of Sutton

DUNGENESS

'The small shed' at Dungeness, which sheltered H. G. Alexander's parents from the (typically) appalling weather in August 1905. The flimsy matchwood structure contained, amazingly in such a small space, ticket office, general waiting room, ladies' room and lavatory, and outside a gentlemen's lavatory and urinal. The ticket office was later abandoned in favour of the small garden shed-type building on the right, whilst the space vacated became part of an enlarged waiting room.

Thrusting out into the channel the headland 'Dunge-Ness' itself could be a most inhospitable place and the only permanent residents were those engaged on lighthouse, coastguard or Admiralty duties. The signal station operated by the latter is on the left in the background, the 'Admiralty Siding' curving away in front. The curious circular building between the signal station and the lighthouse was the coastguard's quarters.

Lens of Sutton

Wainwright 'H' class 0—4—4T No. 162 prepares to run round its train on 17th October 1929. The 'Admiralty Siding' running through the gate in the background was usually controlled by a ganger working a hand point.

H. C. Casserley

The wholly peculiar setting at 'The Ness'. The 'Admiralty Siding' can be seen following the road to the left, whilst the line curving in the front of the station is the Dungeness Loop of the narrow gauge Romney, Hythe and Dymchurch Railway.

Collection John Wimble

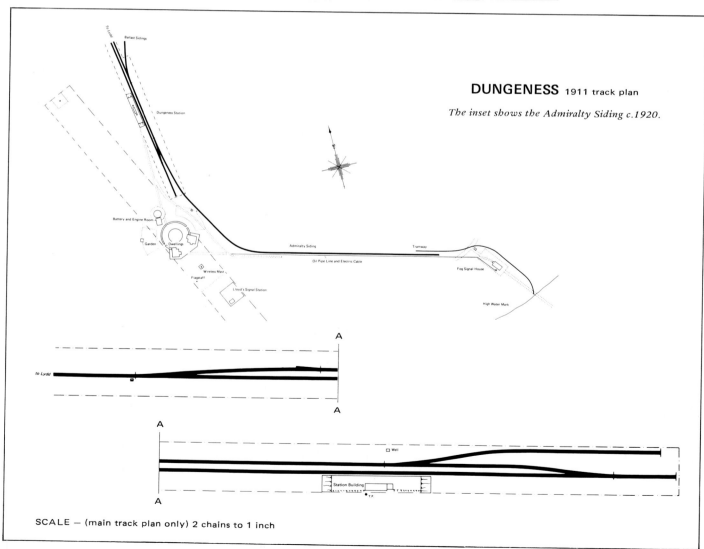

DUNGENESS 1911 track plan

The inset shows the Admiralty Siding c.1920.

To Lydd

Ballast Sidings

Dungeness Station

Battery and Engine Room

Garden   Dwellings

Wireless Mast

Flagstaff

Lloyd's Signal Station

Admiralty Siding

Oil Pipe Line and Electric Cable

Tramway

Fog Signal House

High Water Mark

to Lydd

A

A

A

A

Well

Station Building

SCALE — (main track plan only) 2 chains to 1 inch

A pause while loading parcels at Dungeness in Southern days. The Lydd station master normally accompanied the train to collect tickets and sell them to prospective customers at the terminus. *Lens of Sutton*

'D3' class 0—4—4T No. 2365, before its brush with the Luftwaffe (*see loco notes*), awaits departure to Lydd in the late 1930s. The platforms were faced in wood with an infill of shingle. Like many branches in the south-east of England, the New Romney line found itself on the 'front line' during hostilities in 1939-45. Mobile armoured guns were placed at several locations over the system during this period, Dungeness acquiring a unit briefly in 1943. In the 1914-18 war, orders were issued that 'blinds must be lowered in carriages which may be observed from the seaward side'. *Lens of Sutton*

74

The 'small shed' at Dungeness before the provision of its miniature ticket office. It is difficult to envisage a lonelier wait, enlivened for these two at least by the activities of the photographer.

H. A. Vallance

'B' class 0—4—4T No. 1675 at Dungeness on Saturday, 3rd July 1937, after arrival with the 2.03 p.m. 'push-pull' train from Lydd. The line closed to passengers the following day. A siding leading through the gate in the background served some ballast pits. Known, appropriately enough, as the 'Ballast Siding', it was controlled by the train staff and was worked only under 'special service', with points, etc. operated by a ganger.

R. F. Roberts

The view to Lydd the same day, across the flat and lonely expanse of the Denge Marsh.

R. F. Roberts

LYDD-ON-SEA

The new alignment, intended to serve holiday camps, homes and hotels, opened on 4th July 1937. The old curve and junction were abandoned and a station built on the new alignment to replace passenger facilities removed from Dungeness itself. The new junction was much nearer to the latter and it was felt that those few customers still desirous of visiting Dungeness could do so from the new halt, 'Lydd-on-Sea', a mile and a half away across the shingle. The mixed train passing the station on 18th June 1958 was in fact a St. Leonards shed duty. It usually ran as a passenger train from Ashford to New Romney and on arrival the loco would shunt New Romney yard. On the return journey the wagons could be detached at Lydd, an Ashford engine shunting the yard and returning them to Ashford. *H. C. Casserley*

The beckoning but illusory holiday traffic meant the original plans were far more extensive than those which finally emerged. Proposals in 1937 had envisaged a large wooden station building with canopy, booking hall, etc. A somewhat disappointing wooden shed was all that appeared, but of the original large-scale scheme a run round loop, footbridge and platform of main line dimensions did emerge. A relatively large car park, designed to cope with a fleet of motor buses, was also built, the Southern clinging to its holiday camp hopes.

Mr. B. Cope, a former railwayman on the branch, started his career at Lydd-on-Sea in 1939 as a porter/booking clerk. One of his many duties was to light the signal lamps but, he says, 'not to operate them'. From his first days he recalls 'all train crossings were carried out at Lydd, the run-round loop never being used'. Scattered along this part of the coast were several old coaches, occupied by retired persons; one of Mr. Cope's tasks was to pay out their weekly pensions and, unofficially, to collect freshly caught fish for train crews working the branch. Although 'very bleak indeed in winter', Mr. Cope recalls the station master at Lydd 'exercising his dog in all weathers. He used to visit the station once a week', usually being observed from the footbridge. During the war the area was restricted; all the staff being issued with passes. He recalls helping out at Appledore for a short period and whilst at Lydd the station was attacked several times. He received his call-up papers in 1940.

R. F. Roberts

The run round loop had only very limited use, and by 1954 was probably even more weed-covered than the hopelessly incongruous platform. In that year it was proposed to remove both the loop and the footbridge, its timbers having suffered particularly in the driving rains and icy winters of the marsh. Its main RSJ was in fact secondhand, having been recovered during alterations at New Cross Gate in 1935. The trek to the point at this time must have seemed particularly uninviting and the bold few who gave thought to visiting Dungeness by rail must have rapidly reconsidered their plans after 1937.

Lens of Sutton

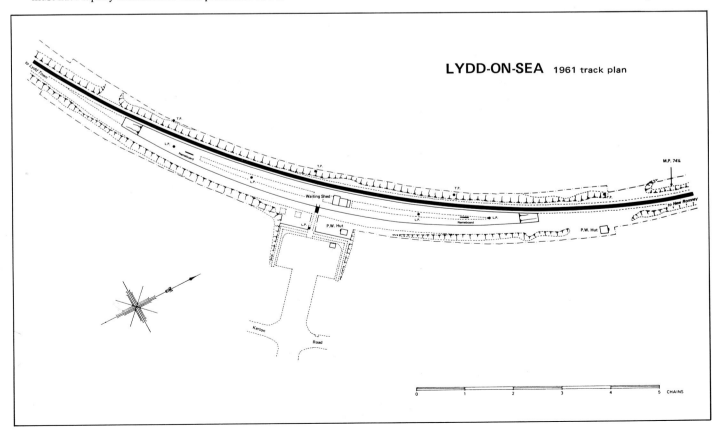

LYDD-ON-SEA 1961 track plan

The diesel sets did little to enliven the prospect, but a few modern houses are visible in this 1965 photograph. *Alan A. Jackson*

GREATSTONE-ON-SEA

Greatstone-on-Sea Halt was the second station on the Southern's new line and exhibited similar expectations and disappointments. Although lacking a run round loop, the platform was once again of generous length and an extensive coach park was provided outside. The corrugated hut was originally envisaged as a wooden building standing on a concrete plinth 63 feet in length. 2–6–2T No. 84029 arrives on 9th June 1960, the advertisement, too late, proclaiming the presence of 'Maddiesons Holiday Camp'.

T. Wright

GREATSTONE-ON-SEA 1961 track plan

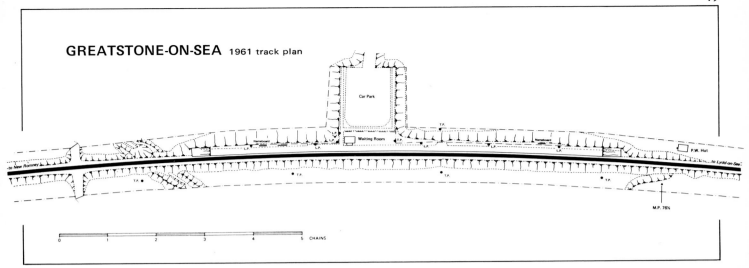

As at Lydd-on-Sea, incidental items, lamp posts, fences, etc. were executed in concrete, at the Exmouth Junction Works of the Southern. *Lens of Sutton*

Greatstone-on-Sea Halt on 28th September 1955, looking towards New Romney.

D. Thompson

The old SER alignment near New Romney, looking north on 3rd July 1937. The as yet unconnected 'junction' with the new 'coast' line lies around the curve, with the new line signal ready for use on the extreme right.
R. F. Roberts

The signal itself, on 3rd July 1937, with the old line trailing in from the left and everything in readiness for connection the next day.
R. F. Roberts

Looking north from the same point in July the following year, the old line on the right having been removed and fenced off. The site was some ¾ mile from New Romney, by Greatstone Golf Links.
R. F. Roberts

80

NEW ROMNEY

The attractive single platform station at New Romney on 23rd March 1940. The grass-clad example on the right originally formed a second platform but for many years served as a livestock loading dock. The pleasing array of wrought iron lamps lasted, fortunately, through to dieselisation. The engine is ex-LBSC 'D3' 0—4—4T No. 2363, awaiting departure on the 1.30 p.m. ex-Ashford, arriving at New Romney at 2.18 p.m.

R. F. Roberts

Station forecourt in the 1950s.

Lens of Sutton

The terminus on 23rd March 1940. The small signal box, conforming to usual SER practice, went out of use in the 1950s. After closure a shunter or guard was expected to carry out the necesssary point movements from the 'closed' box, all signals having been removed. A small water tank for many years stood at the platform end, perched in increasingly precarious fashion on a pile of sleepers.   *R. F. Roberts*

Passenger work was principally in the charge of small pre-Grouping tanks throughout Southern and early BR days. Ex-LBSC 'D3' class 0—4—4T No. 32368 (originally No. 368 *Newport*) leaves New Romney with the 5.50 p.m. for Ashford on 13th May 1950.

Collection J. Scrace

NEW ROMNEY 1961 track plan

The prospect on departure from Lydd, March 1940. In addition to the improvised water tower was a makeshift loading gauge, a double unit obtained from elsewhere and converted.

R. F. Roberts

The disparate pre-Grouping 0—4—4Ts were largely replaced when new standard designs became available, more powerful and capable of a much greater range of duties. First of these were Fairburn-designed 2—6—4Ts constructed at Brighton, and here No. 42096, of the 1950 batch, inches its way past the goods shed on Saturday, 28th June 1952. These locos were very popular with the crews, being 'much more comfortable', with seats and sliding windows. Coal was dumped by this siding so that crews could replenish the bunkers if necessary and is here quite clearly in two separate grades.

R. F. Roberts

The SER lengthened the platform in the 1880s, the change in fencing marking the extent of the work. The various differences in the style of the platform itself, etc., are apparent in both photographs taken on 23rd March 1940.
R. F. Roberts

SECR wrought iron elegance at New Romney in 1964, surviving the rigours of time to greet the diesels, harbingers of closure. The eccentric water tower had long given way to a brick-built example, and the accompanying signal box had also been swept away. The last day of regular steam working appears to have been 25th February 1962 when an 'H' class 0—4—4T and a 'C' class 0—6—0 hauled a special, 'The Kentish Venturer', to New Romney.
R. T. H. Platt

'New Romney and Littlestone-on-Sea' before its prosperity waned. All is smart and clean, not least the splendid 'H' class tank, No. 1512.
Lens of Sutton

A train crew poses alongside the cab of 'D3' class No. 2363 waiting to take out the 3.01 p.m. Ashford train, on Saturday, 23rd March 1940.
R. F. Roberts

New Romney in 1950. The wooden waiting shelter to the left of the main station building was added in 1901 and included a lamp store. The small corrugated iron hut at the far end of the platform housed the oil supply for the station. *L & GRP courtesy David & Charles*

The Drewry pentrol engine railcar awaiting return to Appledore. This vehicle was an early attempt at branch line economy and ultimately a failure, not least in terms of passenger comfort! *Dr. I. C. Allen*

Stirling 7 ft 4—4—0 No. 1151 (originally class 'F' but rebuilt by Wainwright to 'F1') conventionally tender first on a 'down' working at New Romney on 14th June 1936. *S. W. Baker*

Eventide departure in the summer of 1958, the branch now in its fading years. The RHDR, destined to become the only railway serving the town, runs in the cutting on the left, crossing Station Road by an underbridge.
H. C. Casserley

An early postcard view entitled 'Railway Station, Littlestone-on-Sea'.
Lens of Sutton

In 1927 the Southern Railway extended the line through the gate and across 'Station Road' into the narrow gauge premises of the Romney, Hythe and Dymchurch Railway, forming an exchange siding. Traffic, most notably coal for the RHDR locomotives was, like at other sidings on the branch, subject to detailed regulations: 'New Romney/RHDR Siding exchange. Controlled by New Romney box. When required Scotch Blocks and keys to gate kept in New Romney Ground Frame. Exchange traffic must be made in day-light by the company's engine, but before movement across Station Road can commence arrangements must be made to have a Light Railway member present. An SR employee must be stationed on the road with red and green flags. There must not be more than four trains in any one day.'

In March 1950, the Duke of Sutherland's 0—4—4T *Dunrobin* with accompanying saloon coach, was an unusual visitor to the branch. Running in steam from its previous home in Golspie, Scotland to Carlisle, she was towed to Ashford shed. The final run from Ashford to New Romney was again completed under her own steam. *Dunrobin* was housed in a specially constructed shed on the exchange siding and was periodically displayed alongside the RHDR locomotives. She was sold in 1965 to a Canadian businessman and is now on display in a British Columbian museum.

Ken Nunn, courtesy L.C.G.B.

'Littlestone-on-Sea' in 1967, the branch's final year. The first notions of closure had come in November 1965, with the *Kentish Express* running an item headlined 'Closedown Threat on the Ponderosa Line'. Erroneously describing 'the end-of-line station' as dating from 1862, it reported only two regular London commuters using the station, 'which averages between 40 to 50 travellers on a good day'. Mr. Bill Wozencroft of Greatstone ran New Romney single-handed, as porter/guard/ticket-collector/clerk. Such flexibility failed to impress. The branch closed on 6th March 1967 (although the original date was to be 9th January, there was a delay in obtaining a replacement bus service) apart 'from the section of line between Appledore and Lydd . . . . in connection with the nuclear power station and for removal of atomic waste.'

In the event it also remains open for ballast traffic. The suggested replacement buses where they materialized at all, have of course long since disappeared. The Mayor of Folkestone, Councillor Captain W. E. Lawrence, certainly expressed hopes that more buses would appear, but in central London, to assist holidaymakers from the Midlands in reaching the Folkestone area. A 1965 interview records 'although he did not know much about freight, he believed that sugar beet growers would feel the difference'. Obviously a student of transport, he went on: 'After listening to Dr. Beeching on the radio I think he is a man who is in command of the situation'.

E. Wilmshurst

1919 Working Timetable, dated March 1st, 'and until further notice'

ASHFORD, HASTINGS, APPLEDORE AND NEW ROMNEY LINES.

WEEK DAYS—Down Trains.

		a.m.	a.m.	a.m.	a.m.		a.m.	a.m.	p.m.	p.m.	p.m.		p.m.	p.m.	p.m.	p.m.	p.m.		p.m.
Ashford	dep.			8 17			11 2			12 55				4 5			6 13		
Ham Street	arr.			8 26			11 11			T1 3				T4 14			6 22		
Appledore {	arr.			8 32			11 17			1 9				4 20			6 28		
	dep.			8 37			11 20			1 11				4 23			6 32		
Single Line. Appledore	dep.	7 10			9 50	Steam Rail Car.	11 25	Steam Rail Car.	Mixed Train when required.	1 20		Steam Rail Car.		4 26	Steam Rail Car.		6 41		8 10
Brookland	arr.	7 15			9 55		11 30			1 25				4 31			6 46		8 15
Lydd	"	7 24	8 22		10 4		11 39			1 36				4 40			6 55		8 24
New Romney	"		8 30		10 14		11 49			2 0				4 49			7 5		
Lydd	dep.	7 26	Stop						2 45										
Dungeness	arr.	7 38							2 57										
Rye {	arr.	Stop		8 49			11 29			1 21		Stop		4 34			6 42		Stop
	dep.			8 51			11 31	12 37		1 23			2 30	4 38		5 15	6 45		
Winchelsea	arr.			8 55		10 36	11 35	12 41		T1 27			2 35	4 42		5 20	T6 49		
Snailham Halt	"					10 40							2 42			5 27			
Doleham Halt	"				Depart Lydd 10.6 a.m.	10 47		12 47½					2 48			5 33			
T. Oaks & Gstlg Hlt.	"					10 53		12 53½					2 53			5 38			
Ore	"			9 9		10 58		12 58½					3 4	4 58		5 49	7 7		
Hastings	"			9 16		11 9	11 50	1 10		1 43			3 10	5 3		5 55	7 13		

WEEK DAYS—Down Trains—contd. | | SUNDAYS (And Good Friday)—Down Trains.

		p.m.	p.m.	p.m. SO	p.m.			a.m.	p.m.
Ashford	dep.		9 20					11 7	9 25
Ham Street	arr.		9 28					11 16	9 34
Appledore {	arr.		9 34					11 22	9 40
	dep.		9 37					11 25	9 42
Single Line. Appledore	dep.	Steam Rail Car. One Class only.		9 41					
Brookland	arr.			9 46					
Lydd	"			9 55					
New Romney	"								
Lydd	dep.			Stop	9 57				
Dungeness	arr.				10 9				
Rye {	arr.		9 47		Stop			11 35	9 52
	dep.	8 0	9 50					11 38	9 54
Winchelsea	arr.	8 5	T9 54					11 42	9 58
Snailham Halt	"	8 12							
Doleham Halt	"	8 18							
T. Oaks & Gstlg. Hlt.	"	8 23							
Ore	"	8 34	10 12					11 57	10 13
Hastings	"	8 40	10 18					12 2	10 18

WEEK DAYS. Up Trains.

		a.m.	a.m.	a.m.	a.m. NM	a.m. MO	a.m.	a.m.	p.m.	p.m.	p.m.	p.m.	p.m.	p.m.	p.m.	p.m.		p.m.
Hastings	dep.	6 25		8 25	9 5	9 5		11 28	12 25	1 40		3 30		4 0	5 40		6 55
Ore	arr.	6 29		8 30				11 32	12 29	1 45		3 34		4 5			7 0
T. Oaks & Gstlg. Hlt.	"			8 41				11 43½		1 56				4 16			7 11
Doleham Halt	"			8 45				11 47½		2 0				4 20			7 15
Snailham Halt	"			8 50				11 52½		2 5				4 25			7 30
Winchelsea	"	6 44		8 57	S 9 19			11 59	12 44	2 12				4 32	5 54		7 27
Rye {	"	6 49		9 3	9 27	9 27		12 5	12 50	2 18		T3 49		4 32	5 59		7 33
	dep.	6 52		Stop	9 30	9 30		12 5	12 53			3 55		4 38	6 2		
Single Line. Dungeness	dep.		7 55								3 10	3 59					
Lydd	arr.		8 7								3 22						
New Romney	dep.	6 30	Stop		9 9	9 9	10 40	12 28		2 30	Stop			M5 30			
Lydd	arr.	T6 38			T9 17	T9 17	10 48	12 36		2 38		3 48		K5 40			
Brookland	"	6 48			9 27	9 27	11 2	12 48				3 56		5 57			
Appledore	"	6 53			9 32	9 32	11 7	12 53				4 1		6 3			
Appledore {	arr.	7 2			9 42	9 45		1 3				4 10		6 12			
	dep.	7 7			9 46	9 46		1 7				4 14		6 16			
Ham Street	arr.	7 12			9 51	9 51		1 12				4 19		6 21			
Ashford	"	7 23			10 2	10 2		1 23				4 30		6 32			

WEEK DAYS. Up Trains—contd. | | SUNDAYS (And Good Friday)—Up Trains.

		p.m.	p.m.	p.m. SO				a.m.	a.m.	p.m.
Hastings	dep.	7 30						6 50	9 53	5 32
Ore	arr.	T7 34						6 54	9 57	5 36
T. Oaks & Gstlg. Hlt.	"									
Doleham Halt	"								10 5	
Snailham Halt	"									
Winchelsea	"	7 49						7 9	10 15	5 51
Rye {	"	7 54						7 14	10 19	5 56
	dep.	7 57						7 16	10 20	5 58
Single Line. Dungeness	dep.			10 15						
Lydd	arr.			10 27						
New Romney	dep.	7 35	9 0							
Lydd	arr.	T7 43	T9 8	Stop						
Brookland	"	7 54	9 20							
Appledore	"	7 59	9 25							
Appledore {	arr.	8 9						7 28	10 31	6 10
	dep.	8 13						7 30	10 33	6 13
Ham Street	arr.	T8 18						7 35		6 17
Ashford	"	8 30						7 46	10 45	6 27

G Mixed Trip Appledore to New Romney.   **K** Depart Lydd 5.47 p.m.   **L** Depart Lydd 12.40 p.m.
M Mixed Train New Romney to Appledore.   **N** Depart Lydd 1.50 p.m.   **R** Depart Lydd 10.53 a.m.
S Will call at Winchelsea by signal, when required to pick up Passengers, **on Tuesdays.**   (T 3/47756 T.P.)
T Two minutes allowed at these Stations.   ‡ Depart Lydd 9.12 p.m.

New Romney portion of the 6.28 Ashford-Rye train separated and ready for branch duties on 28th June 1952. *R. F. Roberts*

LOCOMOTIVES & OPERATIONAL NOTES

Numerous and varied were the locomotives employed on the Lydd Railway, predominantly tender types in earlier years, tanks subsequently taking over the passenger services. The locomotives, working invariably tender first from Lydd, were provided exclusively from Ashford in pre-Grouping days, the advent of the Southern bringing increasing visits by ex-LBSC locos on St. Leonards diagrams. One locomotive and train sufficed for most of the services, securing the necessary economies and bringing about the Brookland pantomime, described more fully on page 61. Lydd trains either ran through to Ashford or connected with Ashford trains at Appledore. H. P. White (*Forgotten Railways of South East England* published by David & Charles) records eight weekday departures from Appledore in 1905. Four served both New Romney and Dungeness, four Dungeness only. The only Sunday working was a return trip to New Romney. Sunday services were suspended from 1st January 1917 and not restored (June–September only) until 1927. During the 'thirties they commenced in early May but were once again abandoned, as a wartime economy, from 1940 until 1949.

The Stirling 'A', 'B' and 'F' classs 4—4—0s gave way to tank engines after the Grouping, ex-Brighton 'D1' 0—4—2Ts and 'D3' 0—4—4Ts with ex-SECR 'H' 0—4—4Ts. 'C' class 0—6—0s were frequently seen on freights and appear to have been the last steam types employed on the line. Ashford engines Nos. 31272 and 31280 were at work on snow plough duties on New Year's Day 1963. Only one other 'C' was active by this time.

Rebuilt Wainwright 'F1' class 4—4—0 prepares to leave for Appledore on 17th October 1929. *H. C. Casserley*

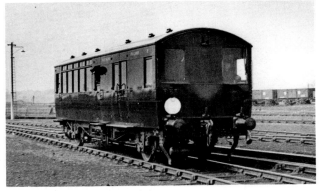

The Drewry railcar arriving on shed at Ashford in March 1933, having just worked the afternoon services on the New Romney line. *Dr. I. C. Allen*

At odd times, various locomotives visited the line on suitability trials. 'P' class 0—6—0T No. 753 ran brief trials when new around 1910, following railcars Nos. 1 and 8 similarly employed when new. No. 8 ran from 1906 to 1907. The SECR 'Terrier' No. 751, purchased in 1904 (later Carriage Works shunter), also visited the line on trial on 29th January 1910. After the Second World War KESR No. 3 appeared for a film company.

A four-wheel Drewry petrol railcar was also tried on the New Romney line. Built in 1927, its engine was uprated at Ashford in 1930 from 50 to 64 hp. A 'singularly uncomfortable' vehicle, in 1930 its seating capacity was reduced from 26 to 22.

A 1920s account of the branch services:

As showing the usual traffic arrangements which apply on these branches, it may be pointed out that, during the summer months, the services of the engine provided for dealing with goods traffic are utilised to enable the New Romney and Dungeness branches to be served from Lydd independently. This applies, however, only during the morning period, and for the first service each way. Thus commencing at Appledore at 7.7 a.m., there are trains from Lydd to Dungeness at 7.23 a.m. and to New Romney at 7.29 a.m., returning, respectively, at 7.40 and 7.56 a.m. One of the trains returns to Appledore, while the other remains at Lydd until 8.25, when it goes to New Romney. Then the sequence of journeys is as follows:-

New Romney	.. ..	9.15	10.35	11.58
Appledore	.. ..	9.39	11.02	12.21
Appledore	.. ..	9.55	11.21	1.00
New Romney	.. ..	10.19	11.46	1.37

So far, Dungeness has been disregarded since the first trip, but Dungeness has to be given a connection with the 1.0 p.m. from Appledore, so the train returns from New Romney at 2.0 p.m. to Lydd, and at 2.13 p.m. takes Dungeness passengers, who have been waiting since 1.17 p.m. Back again at 1.33 p.m.

BR standard 2—6—2T No. 84028 takes water at New Romney on 10th June 1960. Modern tank types ousted the old 0—4—4Ts in the 1950s, first arrivals being the Brighton-built 2—6—4s of LMS design. BR 2—6—2Ts and 2—6—4Ts took over when these were transferred to the LMR. *T. Wright*

New Year's Day 1963, with two 'C' 0—6—0s, Nos. 31271 and 31280. *G. A. Barlow*

The branch was the scene of perhaps the most remarkable wartime incident on a British railway, a circumspect account appearing in the *Sunday Dispatch* of 1942:

'How my engine got a Nazi' by the Driver — 27/11/42. The driver of the first locomotive to bring down a German aeroplane yesterday told the story of his strange adventure to the *Sunday Dispatch*. He is Mr. C. Gilbert, and his home is in Ashford in Kent. The incident happened as he was pulling his train out of a small coastal station. 'I did not know that a Focke-Wulf fighter plane was less than 20 ft above until I heard a burst of cannon-fire which caused the boiler to burst, and I was blown through the air onto the embankment. It was all smoke and fire, water and steam, and bits of metal flying in all directions. I was lucky to escape without any injury!' The pilot and remains of his plane were located some 100 yards up the track, the pilot having died in the explosion. The 'plane had previously attacked an inland area and had killed a farm worker.'

D3 0—4—4T 2365 returned to service after repair at Ashford 11th March the following year. *British Railways, courtesy R. C. Riley*

to Lydd only and at 2.55 p.m. to New Romney, another sequence is started:-

New Romney	..	..	3.12	5.30	7.40
Appledore	..	..	3.36	6.02	8.08
Appledore	..	..	4.40	6.43	—
New Romney	..	..	5.04	7.06	—

Next, except on Saturdays, the train runs from Appledore at 8.15 p.m. to Dungeness, returning at 9.0 p.m. to Appledore. Then at 9.56 to Lydd, with a late train on Wednesdays and Fridays to New Romney and back to Lydd, finishing there at 10.42 p.m. On Saturdays, however, the 8.15 p.m. from Appledore goes to Lydd only, thence back to Appledore at 9.25 p.m.,

at 9.56 to Lydd and through to Dungeness instead of New Romney, and so back to Lydd at 10.47 p.m., continuing as a fast train through to Ashford, leaving Lydd at 11.10 p.m. and not calling even at Appledore. As there are no Sunday trains on either branch, this is, presumably, to bring the engine to Ashford for shed day and attention. Truly a peculiar way of working, but apparently quite suited to the needs of this strange locality, especially as New Romney and Littlestone get a fairly good service of trains well distributed over the day, and Dungeness has quite sufficient facilities for its inevitably meagre traffic. Usually a tender engine is used on these services, as it is able to carry sufficient water for several journeys without possible delays from that cause, though it does half its running tender first.

Instructions from 1919 SECR Passenger Working Book

INSTRUCTIONS TO ENGINEMEN AND GUARDS WORKING TRAINS TO AND FROM THE DUNGENESS BRANCH.

To Dungeness.—Before leaving Lydd the Signalman must hand to the Driver the Occupation Key, which the Driver will accept as his authority to proceed over the Single Line as far as Romney Junction. On arrival at this place, the Driver must stop short of the Junction Points and hand the Key to the Guard, who must insert same in the Lock of Ground Frame, giving one turn to unlock the Controlling Lever. The Guard must then set and Bolt the Points for the Branch and give the Driver a Hand-Signal for Train to draw forward on to Branch, clear of the Main Line (Lydd to New Romney). As soon as the Train is clear, the Guard must restore the Points for Main Line, withdraw Key from Ground Frame, and insert the Key in the Occupation Key Instrument which is fixed in the Ground Frame Box. The Guard must turn the Key from "3" to "1" (thereby permitting Tablet Working on Main Line) and advise the Signalman at Lydd by telephone (which is also fixed in Ground Frame Box) when this is done. Train must then proceed to Dungeness.

The Occupation Key must on no account be placed in the Occupation Key Instrument until the whole of the Train has been drawn on to Dungeness Branch, clear of Main Line.

Returning from Dungeness.—On arrival at Romney Junction, Engine Driver must stop at the Branch Home Signal. Guard must proceed to Ground Frame Box and—
(A) Advise Lydd by Telephone that he requires the Occupation Key;
(B) Turn the Key Instrument to "2";
(C) Wait until Indicator shows "Free." When Indicator shows "Free" the Guard must turn the Occupation Key from "2" to "3," withdraw the Key and insert it in Lock of Ground Frame, unlock Controlling Lever, set Points and Lower Signal. Train to be then drawn on to Main Line clear of Junction Points. As soon as the Train is clear, the Signal and Points must be restored to their normal position and Key withdrawn from Ground Frame and handed to Driver.
Train can then proceed to Lydd, and on arrival Key must be handed to the Signalman.

INSTRUCTIONS TO SIGNALMEN.

To withdraw Key at Lydd.—The Tablet Instruments must be at normal. Having satisfied himself as to this, the Signalman at Lydd must turn Occupation Key Instrument to "2," and give the Bell Signal (5—2, see B.T. Rule 13) to New Romney; the latter, when acknowledging, to hold the Plunger in on the last beat until Indicator Needle drops to the vertical (normal) position. On the last beat the Switch Instrument at Lydd must be turned to "2," and the Indicator of same will show "Free." Switch must then be turned from "2" to "4," which will drop the Indicator of Occupation Key Instrument to "Free," and enable the Occupation Key to be turned from "2" to "3" and withdrawn. Switch must then be turned back to "3" and Occupation Key given to Engine Driver.

To restore Key at Lydd.—Key must be inserted in Occupation Key Instrument and turned to "1." Switch can then be turned to "1" and Tablet Working is restored. The Signalman at Lydd must then send the Bell Signal 2—5 to New Romney.

The Single Line Regulations and Train Staff for the working between Romney Junction and Dungeness and controlling Waterworks Siding and Ground Frame at Dungeness will remain in operation as formerly, except that the Train Staff must be exchanged at Lydd instead of at Romney Junction.

To withdraw Key at Romney Junction.—The Guard will Telephone Signalman at Lydd and turn Occupation Key Instrument to "2." The Signalman at Lydd, having satisfied himself that the Tablet Instruments are at normal, must give the Bell Signal 5—2 to New Romney. The Signalman at New Romney, when acknowledging, must hold Plunger in on last beat until Indicator Needle drops to the vertical (normal) position. On the last beat the Switch Instrument at Lydd must be turned to "2" and the Indicator of same will show "Free." The Switch must then be turned from "2" to "4," which will drop the Indicator of Occupation Key Instrument at Romney Junction to "Free," enabling the key to be turned by the Guard from "2" to "3" and withdrawn.

To restore Key at Romney Junction.—When the Key is inserted in Occupation Key Instrument at Romney Junction and turned from "3" to "1," it will show "Free" on the Indicator in Switch Instrument at Lydd. Switch at Lydd must then be turned to "1," which will restore Tablet Working. The Signalman at Lydd must then send the Bell Signal 2—5 to New Romney.

BROOKLAND STATION BUILDING

R E A R   E L E V A T I O N

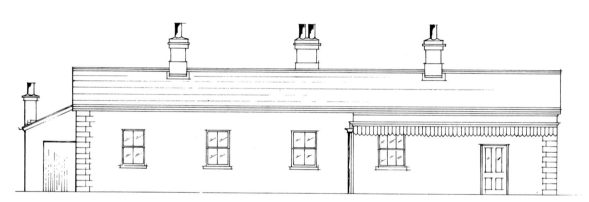

E L E V A T I O N   T O   P L A T F O R M

P L A N

SCALE — 2 mm to 1 foot

DUNGENESS STATION BUILDING

E L E V A T I O N   T O   P L A T F O R M

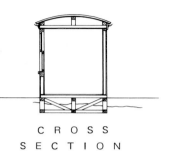

C R O S S
S E C T I O N

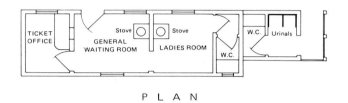

| TICKET OFFICE | | GENERAL WAITING ROOM | Stove | Stove | LADIES ROOM | W.C. | W.C. | Urinals | |

P L A N

SCALE — 2 mm to 1 foot

LYDD-ON-SEA STATION FOOTBRIDGE

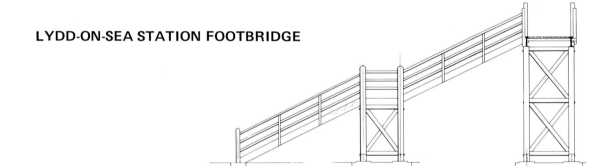

S I D E   E L E V A T I O N

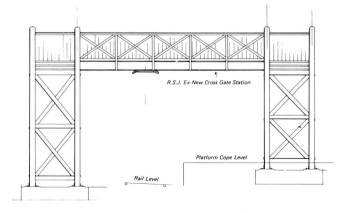

R.S.J. Ex-New Cross Gate Station

Platform Cope Level

Rail Level

F R O N T   E L E V A T I O N

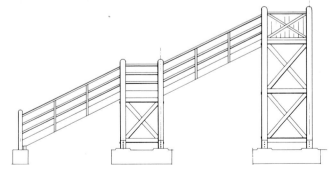

S I D E   E L E V A T I O N

SCALE — 2 mm to 1 foot

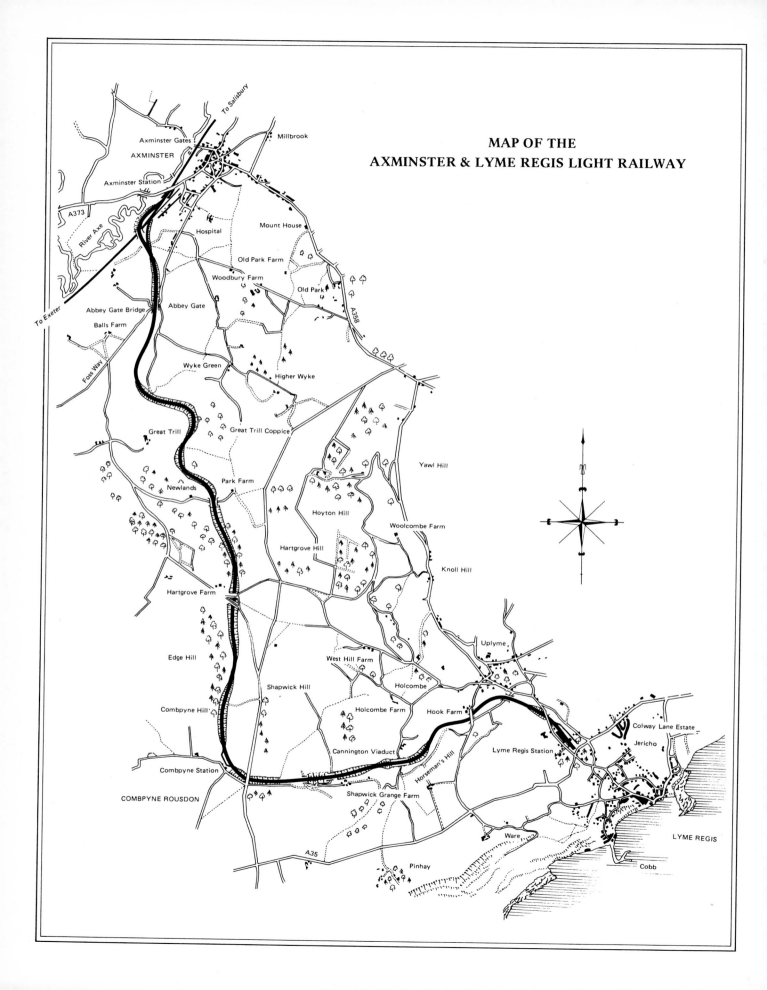

**MAP OF THE
AXMINSTER & LYME REGIS LIGHT RAILWAY**

The Axminster & Lyme Regis Light Railway

LYME REGIS was typical of many branch lines in the south west of England, in its complex pre-construction history. An endless procession of broadly similar schemes were floated, fought and lost over nearly sixty years when the little resort, afraid of economic stagnation, struggled to become connected to the increasingly important national railway network. The Axminster and Lyme Regis Light Railway was not finally opened until 24th August 1903 and it would be difficult and probably tedious in an account of this nature to detail all the political and economic twists since the first proposal emerged in 1845.

Not the least of the obstacles facing the line was, surprisingly enough, the London & South Western Railway itself. The company had been more than ready to support proposals for a branch to Lyme in the early 1870s but as soon as the main purpose of this had been achieved, that of thwarting the GWR, it showed little further interest. The LSWR effectively 'killed' proposals for a line on three occasions, once in the 1860s (together with the Great Western) and twice in the 1880s. A plea in 1898, in the form of a petition containing nearly 2,000 signatures, was once again ignored, and it took the committed involvement of a local notary, Sir Wilfred Peek, for the LSWR to finally agree to the construction of a new line. Sir Wilfred's influence and an application by the promoters to the Light Railway Commissioners at last forced the recalcitrant LSWR to accept the idea of a branch to Lyme Regis.

The nearest Lyme had come to gaining its longed for railway during the nineteenth century was in 1874, when matters advanced as far as a sod-cutting ceremony, followed by a banquet, etc. The LSWR had actually been persuaded in 1871 to agree to work a line (for half the receipts) if one could be constructed. The company was still nervous about potential Great Western incursions and this is certainly the only reason its support for a branch was forthcoming. The Bill for a Lyme Regis Railway Company to connect with the LSWR at Axminster was passed by Parliament in the summer of 1871 and the abortive first sod was cut on 29th September 1874, in an atmosphere of public holiday and rejoicing at Lyme. Optimism was such that plans were deposited with Parliament for enlargements at the proposed Lyme Regis

station and an extension of the line along the coast to Bridport. Remarkably no further action ensued and to the satisfaction of the LSWR the powers lapsed.

To return to 1898, the good townsfolk, enthusiastic as ever, felt that by now the hand of the obdurate LSWR might at last be forced, and indeed in this they were to prove correct. Under the Axminster and Lyme Regis Light Railway Order of 15th June 1899 powers were granted for a line from the station at Axminster to a site about half a mile from the town centre at Lyme.

At last when the line was finally complete the LSWR could express some measure of contrition:

> It was impossible to connect Lyme Regis with the railway system of the country without engineering works of considerable magnitude; but the facilities offered by the Light Railway Act, and the skill of Mr. Arthur C. Pain, M.Inst.C.E., who has made a special study of this class of undertaking, have at last brought the expense of a line to Lyme Regis within practicable limits.

Construction had begun in June 1900 aided by a subscription of £25,000 from the LSWR. Difficulties were experienced in the work (much of the heavier material was landed by sea at Lyme) and an extension of the Light Railway Order was required.

> The Cannington Valley viaduct is the great feature of the new railway from an engineering point of view; in fact, it may be said to have rendered the whole undertaking practicable by making unnecessary the tunnel involved in most previous schemes. A few years ago, indeed, the latter might have been considered preferable from the economic standpoint; but the modern practice of using mass concrete in bridge-building has very greatly reduced the cost of such structures; and, in the case of the viaduct in question, crushed flints from the adjacent cutting yielded a suitable material for the manufacture of the concrete without the admixture of sand. Moreover, the employment of a cableway, instead of scaffolding, for the erection of the viaduct still further reduced the expense as compared with similar structures of less modern design and execution. On the other hand, the fears of the engineer as to the suitability of the soil of the hills for tunnelling have been confirmed by his experience in one of the cuttings near Lyme Regis, where the treacherous green-sand has slipped persistently, necessitating the sides of the cutting being supported by a timber breastwork with a backing of corrugated iron sheets.
>
> Messrs. Baldry and Yerburgh, contractors, Westminster. have carried out the work.

Among the very last of Britain's 'navvies', workmen involved with the new viaduct pose as construction of the final elliptical arch begins. Cannington was of considerable engineering significance with an influence beyond the strictly railway field. As such it provoked considerable interest in contemporary professional journals.

Authors' collection

The construction of the viaduct was also covered by *The Railway Engineer* in 1905:

Construction of a Concrete Railway Viaduct.

The viaduct in question is situated at Cannington, on the Axminster and Lyme Regis Light Railway, which now connects Lyme Regis with the Yeovil and Exeter line of the London and South-Western Railway. It consists of ten elliptical arches of 50 feet span, its total length being 600 feet, width over spandrels 16 feet, maximum height to rail-level 92 feet, and gradient 1 in 80. It affords an example of the recent application of concrete to viaduct construction and to arches of somewhat large span. With the exception of the concrete blocks in the vertical faces of the arches, the work throughout is mass concrete.

The geological strata are greensand and blue lias clay. The foundations, originally designed for a pressure of 3½ tons per square foot, were enlarged to give pressures ranging from 1½ ton to 3 tons per square foot.

The concrete used consisted of crushed flints and Portland cement, the crushing yielding sufficient grit to make the addition of sand unnecessary except in special cases. The concrete was hand-mixed, and for transporting this and other materials a cableway of 1,000 feet span was erected across the valley, the piers being built without scaffolding.

The piers were carried up in rectangular lifts of diminishing size, instead of having a continuous batter, the lifts being 6 feet deep. The concrete was deposited in wooden boxes of this depth, which were bolted up on the ground and hoisted into position. The mode of filling and striking the boxes, which there are eleven, is described. The work in all the piers was advanced as far as possible at the same rate.

Two rows of corbels were built in the top lift of the piers to support the arch-centering. This consisted of four built ribs, the centre portion of which was tied by a framework, in the form of a Warren girder, supported in the middle by raking struts from the lower row of corbels. The ribs, including the lattice-work, were set in one piece, and four tie-bolts were placed in the span to assist the piers in taking the thrust.

The faces of the arches were built in concrete blocks, of which two similar ones on opposite sides of the viaduct were set simultaneously by a rail attachment to the cableway; and by adjusting the chains attaching the blocks the latter were suspended at the angles required by their position in the arch. The blocks were keyed in advance of the mass concrete, in order that the adhesion of the latter to the toothing of the blocks might relieve the centres of some of the weight.

Expansion joints were formed through the arches, spandrels and parapets, and are found effective in giving play for expan-

The viaduct complete, with remedial 'jack arch' safely in place.

Collection K. K. Koraitie

The viaduct became a local landmark of some significance, figuring prominently in the substantial sale of postcards, particularly at Lyme. 'I am taking a quiet walk (alone) up the coast' was the message borne home to Worcester on this card posted on 18th April 1908.

Collection Mrs. F. A. Crawforth

Combpyne, the only intermediate station on the line, new in 1903. Contractors' materials including trolleys, etc. are lying in the background awaiting collection by their owners. Messrs. Baldry and Yerburgh of Westminster were appointed by the promoters to build the line, having tendered at something over £35,000, the engineer being Mr. Arthur C. Pain, M.Inst.C.E., another S.W.1. based professional. Some of the materials used, including cement, Cozens relates, were seaborne, 'offloaded from the ketch *Ida*'. The wagons indicate the early interest shown by the LSWR. A majority of the inspecting party accompanying the Mayor and Major Druitt on the opening of the line were in fact senior officers of the LSWR, including Mr. Holmes, Superintendent at Waterloo. Wagon No. 3796 had been built in 1887, becoming SR Diagram 1301 SR 387 and was withdrawn on 26th October 1929. SR 387 subsequently became 0575S. The next wagon, LSW 11724, built in 1899, became SR Diagram 1595, later 57542, and was withdrawn in August 1934. The original flat bottom rails were later replaced by 90 lb. rail.

Authors' collection

sion and contraction and any slight movement due to settlement. In turning the arches, the centering, although apparently light, was found to be sufficiently rigid, and the setting was facilitated by the ribs being made in one piece.

The settlement of the piers was for the most part fairly even, and, being adjusted as the work proceeded, did not affect the concrete; but the settlement of the west abutment and first pier was greater than elsewhere, and crushed the crown of the first arch. Two diaphragm-walls were built in brickwork in cement in the third span, to enable it to act as an abutment, and concrete needles were built in the embankment between the first and second piers; the crushed portion of the first arch was cut out and made good in brickwork, and the parapets over this arch were completed. Particulars are given of the cost of the viaduct, and a schedule is appended of the results of tests of sample blocks made from materials used in the concrete.

The Authors believe this is the first instance in which piers of a similar height have been built without scaffolding, and in which the centres of a 50-foot arch have been designed for setting in one piece.

A special train ran on 22nd January 1903, following which opening was delayed due to movement in some of the earthworks. Major Druitt of the Board of Trade inspected the works on 21st August and eventually expressed his approval, the line opening three days later on Monday, 24th August 1903, amid general rejoicing, band playing, toasts, speeches and so on.

The initial euphoria was sadly unwarranted and the disappointing traffic, though sufficient to put the local horse-drawn bus and coastal carriers out of business, perhaps somewhat exonerated the LSWR for its previous reticence. Financial difficulties dogged the light railway and on 1st January 1907 the company was entirely absorbed by the LSWR.

Things improved generally after this with agricultural goods, particularly livestock and fertilizer, providing useful business. Excursions proved popular and through trains to the little resort increased steadily. This traffic was severely curtailed by the First World War but resumed in 1919, to be fostered by the Southern in the 'twenties and 'thirties, a Sunday service even appearing in the summer of 1930.

Buses had ominously appeared in the 1920s and by the early 'fifties increasing numbers of private cars were also eroding the local traffic. Excursions continued to sustain the line in summer but the usual story of hopelessly uneconomic traffic levels through the winter was only too apparent.

The inconvenient siting of the terminus, high above and a not inconsiderable distance from the town centre, did not help the situation and the prospect of closure loomed ever nearer. Freight services were withdrawn in early 1964 and, despite the usual protests, the line finally closed on 29th November 1965. The line had drawn railway enthusiasts for some years, with the prolonged use of the ancient Adams 'Radials', but again most visited in the summer and many of these probably travelled by car. The track remained more or less intact for a while but was torn up and sold for scrap in the latter half of 1967.

Garlands and smiles at Lyme Regis on the opening day, with specially purchased ex-LBSC 'Terriers' numbered 734 and 735.   *Collection R. C. Riley*

The simple terminus of the Lyme Regis Light Railway, 1903, perched high on the chalk hillside overlooking the village. The platforms, some 300 ft in length, are in original condition, ballast and shingle between wooden retaining walls. In addition the station's enigmatic boulder lies already in place beneath the station nameboard, 'Lyme Regis for Charmouth'. No satisfactory explanation has emerged for this strange talisman, which remained at Lyme for many years! The unpretentious station and its environs were described thus shortly after opening: 'The view from this point is a magnificent combination of sea, cliff, and land scenery, embracing the coast from Lyme Regis to Portland, as well as a splendid sweep of rolling meadows and richly-wooded hills. A glance at the photograph previously referred to shows that the station buildings are of the modest character befitting a 'light' railway; and while the splendid scenery can be enjoyed, they do not seriously interfere with the prospect from the main road, which runs just above, and is a favourite promenade for the townspeople and visitors.' The locomotive is 0–6–0T No. 735, one of the ex-LBSCR 'Terriers' formerly numbered 646 *Newington*.

Authors' collection

Part of the official sequence of 1903. No station was complete without a 'hotel' of some description, in the case of Lyme a role fulfilled within a short time by the 'Victoria Hotel', an imposing building erected by the yard entrance. The 'Gentlemen's' was shortly afterwards provided with a glass roof.   *Authors' collection*

All is clean and tidy for the official photographer in 1903, with the terminus in original condition. Through the end door, between enthusiastic excursion notices, was the cloakroom and parcels office, offering a counter service. Through the main door at the front was the booking hall and waiting room beyond. At the far end of the building were the toilets and a ladies waiting room. Constructed entirely in wood, the building happily survived and is now in use on the Mid Hants Railway as a book and model shop.   *Authors' collection*

AXMINSTER

The Axminster 'changeover day' 25th May 1935. This weekly event was carried out with the dash typical of Southern men involved in the West of England connecting operations. Salisbury 'King Arthur' 4—6—0 No. 455 *Sir Lancelot* waits with a 'down' train from Waterloo. An Adams 'Radial' tank, symbolic of the Lyme Regis branch, waits alongside on the 'up' line subsequently to work light for servicing at Exmouth Junction shed. A fresh engine, No. 3125, replacement for No. 3520 and newly-arrived from Exmouth Junction, has already coupled up to the branch set.

H. C. Casserley

'King Arthur' class 4—6—0 No. 768 *Sir Balin* on a 'down' train around 1927.

Collection R. Carpenter

An 'S11' 4—4—0 on an 'up' train approaching Axminster in the late 1920s. *Collection R. Carpenter*

A branch train ready for departure on 31st August 1937, the end of the summer season now (probably thankfully) in sight. Traffic reached incredible peaks on summer Saturdays in the 1930s and, despite a certain post-war recovery, was never again so heavy or prolonged. The marvel is that these hard-worked 'Radials' had over twenty more years work before them when this photograph was taken.

Collection W. A. Camwell

The fine stone bridge carrying the Exeter road over the main line, on 17th July 1958. It survives unaltered today. The branch portion of a 'down' Waterloo train is standing on the 'up' line, about to be shunted across ready to go to Lyme Regis. The LSWR had at one time planned a new siding, of some 520 feet, for the 'down' side, ending at the 'down' platform slope. Difficulties with land acquisition moved the SR to abandon these ideas in 1923.

A. E. West

'Merchant Navy' Pacific No. 35013 *Blue Funnel* storms through Axminster on 4th September 1960. *K. A. Stone*

A wooden waiting shed was provided on the 'up' side at Axminster. Originally a simple 'walk through' affair, on the installation of a new SR water column it was boarded in. Doors were inserted at each end to spare patrons an unexpected soaking. 18th December 1956.

A. E. West

Axminster in April 1958. The footbridge survived a major remodelling proposal of the mid 'thirties but not the singling of the main line over thirty years later. The timber canopy, also a survivor from the first years, lost only the valancing. In appearance it was similar to the entrance canopy (below). The footbridge was installed in the mid 1890s and some fifteen years later in 1911 a proposal arose to erect awnings along the entire 'up' platform. The cost of £850 was considered too much and the project was abandoned.   *D. Thompson*

Axminster station in 1960, almost unchanged from its opening one hundred years previously. Much of the building formed the station master's residence, the small slated porch marking his private entrance. Access to the passenger facilities, booking hall, etc. was through the main canopied entrance. Toilets were provided beneath the glazed area, by the public telephone box.

Horse-drawn buses for many years operated from the station yard, the service to Lyme being an immediate casualty. By the time this fine portrait was executed the railway was under severe pressure, paradoxically from buses. In proposals put forward by the SR in 1923, the building would have been completely demolished, the main buildings straddling the line with access from an enlarged roadbridge. The platform faces were to be increased from three to four, with the branch having direct access to the main line. This grandiose scheme, like many at this time, came to nothing.   *R. C. Riley*

Light Pacific No. **34019** *Bideford* with ten coaches on 'the Brighton' on Sunday, 31st July 1960. The train comprised the 10.47 a.m. ex-Brighton and the 12.27 p.m. from Portsmouth and Southsea, making the 12.50 p.m. from Fareham to Plymouth, running four minutes late. Arrival at Plymouth was due at 6.15 p.m.   *K. A. Stone*

The signal box on 28th June 1957. Of standard LSWR construction, it closed completely on 5th March 1967, along with the sidings on the 'down' side.   *A. E. West*

Top left: The goods shed on 19th May 1966. In the earliest years a single road wooden engine shed had been provided, housing a single shunting engine. As well as coal, etc., most local produce was handled here, including Axminster's famous carpets. A trailing connection had been installed at the head of the yard to allow direct access off the branch, but with two ground frames this was considered inconvenient, staff preferring to use the branch bay and shunt across. Lack of use prompted the LSWR to remove the offending connection in 1915. This proved somewhat rash and to its embarrassment the company found itself in 1921 contemplating the reinstallation of the connection, an expensive matter at £1,335. Consideration was also given for a siding on the same site, to hold eight wagons, as well as a second at a cost of £746 on a site rather nearer to the yard. With Grouping (or worse) ever more likely, the proposals were deemed too expensive for an LSWR purse depleted by war, and they were abandoned. *Top right:* Axminster's robust 4 ton 11 cwt. crane. *Above:* The conventional LSW goods shed erected with the station in 1860. This commodious building originally incorporated a small office. It eventually became too small and inconvenient, a larger office being erected at the eastern end of the building at a cost of £76. The original internal office was subsequently demolished.

Photos: A. E. West

End of summer scene at Axminster, 31st August 1957, with Nos. 30582 and 30583 in attendance.

W. Potter

A branch train ready to leave for the coast on 21st May 1935, with an ex-LSW two-coach set. *H. C. Casserley*

Adams tank No. 30583 by the small coal stage at the very end of the branch bay. Early plans indicate only watering facilities here, the stage not appearing until after 1917. The water tank attracted attention over the years, never proving wholly satisfactory until the provision of a 'Vulcan Hydraulic Pump' in 1921/22. Enlargement of the tank was also considered but abandoned when the new pump proved unexpectedly efficient.
M. E. J. Deane

No. 30584 on 2nd August 1959 about to 'run round' for the return trip to Lyme. A number of eager passengers are about to board the train with part of the leading coach off the platform. Both were properly positioned on arrival, allowing passengers to alight but, in order for the engine to gain the run round loop, the coaches were afterwards advanced a few yards. When once again at the head of its train, the engine would then set back, replacing both coaches in the correct position. Lyme passengers could then safely board all parts of the train.

K. A. Stone

In evening sunshine, No. 30582 runs round a solitary coach on 10th July 1956. Through Waterloo coaches were detached and set into a siding on the 'up' side of the main line, there to await the arrival of a London train, it was then a simple procedure to attach them to the rear of the main line train.

R. C. Riley

No. 30584 in August 1959 ready for departure to Lyme Regis. On the left is the LSWR starter signal, with BR arm, whilst the coach is of SECR origin. It was usual for a porter to collect the branch tablet and take it to the signal box but at busy periods almost anyone, including the signalman himself, would perform this task.

K. A. Stone

No. 3488, smokebox first and thus correctly positioned for a 'down' working, leaves Axminster with the 1.45 p.m. train on 25th June 1949. Behind the centre coach is the home signal, dispensed with in 1960 when the line resumed 'one engine in steam' working. This had been the original mode of operation, electric tablets, with a crossing place at Combpyne appearing later. The concrete spikes are anti-tank devices dating from the invasion scare days of 1940.

Photographer unknown

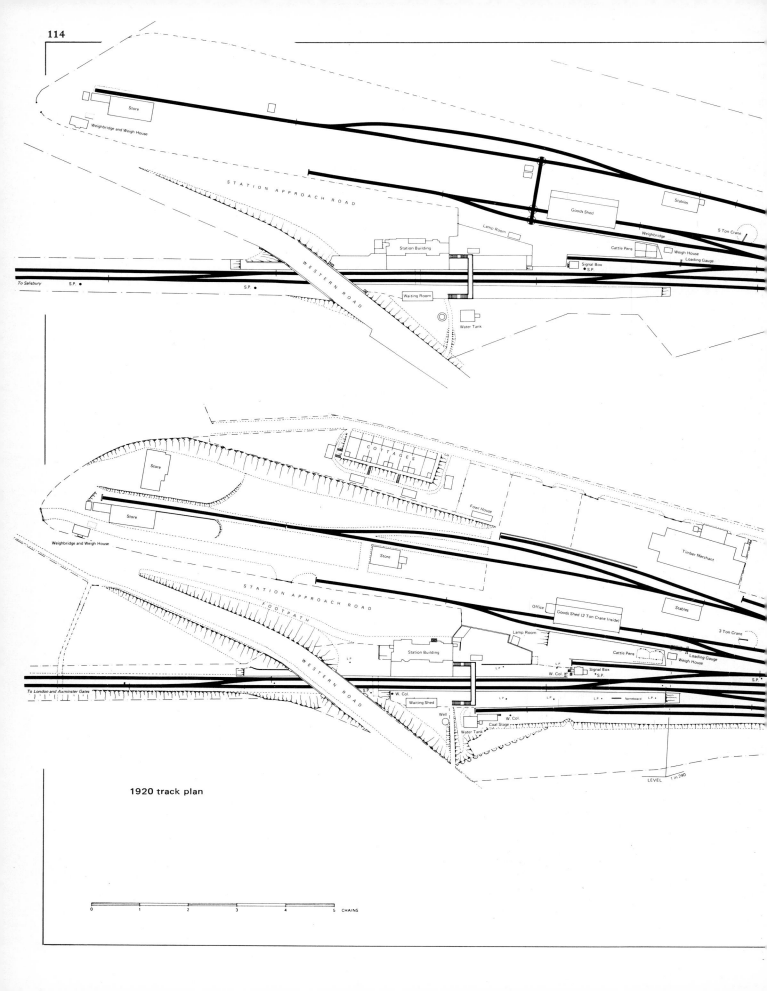

1920 track plan

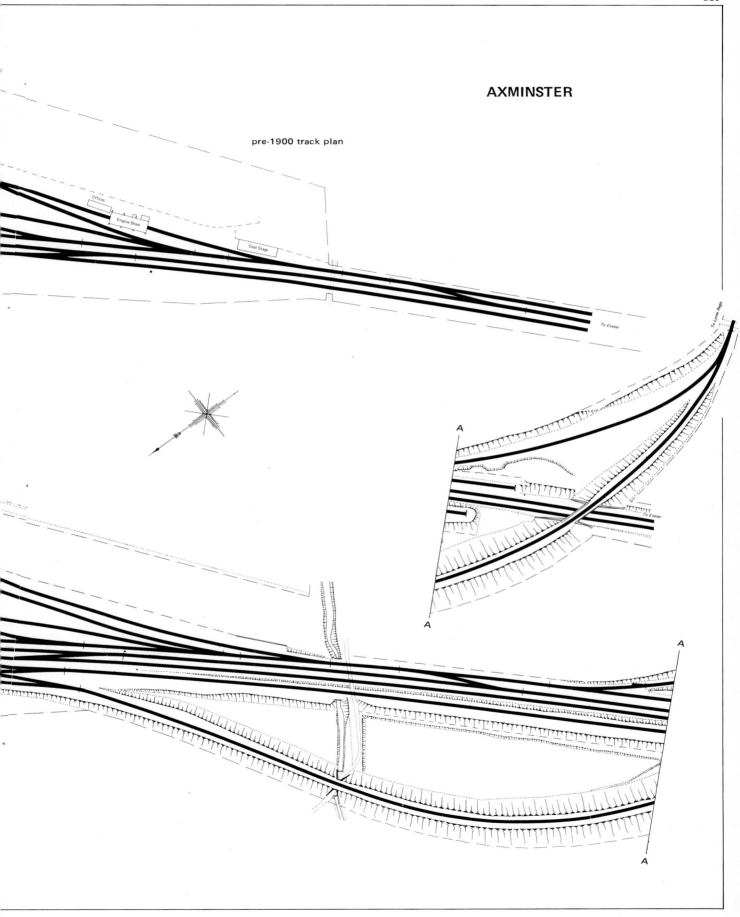

AXMINSTER

pre-1900 track plan

Offices

Engine Shed

Coal Stage

To Exeter

To Lyme Regis

To Exeter

To Lyme Regis

A

A

A

A

The approaches to Axminster, from the iron girder bridge carrying the branch across the main line. In addition to through coaches awaiting attachment to London trains, the 'up' siding on the left frequently held set-back freights. The 'down' siding formed the Axminster yard headshunt, whilst the former trailing connection from the branch is indicated by grassed-over earthwork.

J. E. Gready

'Merchant Navy' Pacific No. 35001 *Channel Packet* speeding through Axminster on 4th September 1960. The lamented 'Atlantic Coast Express' with its multitude of through portions to the various resorts is well known. It was, however, only one of a number of such trains, displaying equally fascinating timetabling accomplishments. The particular duty shown here, No. 526, was the 10.30 a.m. Exeter—Waterloo train, formed from the 8.10 a.m. from Torrington and the 8.53 a.m. from Barnstaple—Exeter. On arrival at Exeter, the 8.25 a.m. Plymouth train was attached and the 10.30 to London was formed. At Sidmouth Junction, further coaches were attached, having themselves undergone some complex workings. They would have begun on the 9.52 a.m. Exmouth—Tipton St. John's train, the engine running round the train at Tipton and setting back in the siding to await the 10.20 train from Sidmouth, to which the Exmouth coaches would be attached. The combined portions proceeded onto Sidmouth Junction, where connection with the 10.30 train from Exeter would be made, the branch train running on to the 'down' main line to await the latter's arrival. Accompanied by a porter/shunter, *Channel Packet* would have detached itself from its train, crossed, picked up the branch coaches, set them back onto the main line train and departed for London, a complex and much underrated procedure accomplished in some five minutes with a minimum of fuss.

K. A. Stone

An 'up' train in the charge of No. 3520 on the 1 in 80 descent to Axminster station on 31st August 1945. Waste ground here served as a dump for permanent way materials and contained an SR locomotive tender off No. 0470, at this time being used as a water tank. *H. C. Casserley*

No. 30584 heading a 'down' train over the severely curved embankment by Trill. *Ivo Peters*

An 'up' train taking the Trill curve on 30th August 1953. *S. C. Nash*

A Lyme Regis train near Bulmoor Cross, winding up through the wooded country around Combpyne to the summit of the line, 470 ft above sea level. There were twenty-seven curves alone of thirty chains or less, and many more less severe. Mechanical lubrication was employed in at least one instance. *Ivo Peters*

A six-coach 'down' train weaves through the woods near Combpyne headed by an 'O2' 0—4—4T, with stovepipe chimney. The locomotive is very probably No. 228, which underwent trials on the branch in 1906. *Collection E. Crawforth*

An 'up' train snakes through the still richly wooded district many years later, on 31st August 1948. Apart from the difficult curves, the Adams tanks were faced with steep gradients on the Lyme Regis branch.

H. C. Casserley

Summer Saturday through trains required double-heading, as on this occasion in the 1950s.

Ivo Peters

The 'English Country Branch' typified in this portrait of No. 30583 near Combpyne on 24th May 1957.

Tony Wright

COMBPYNE

'Combpyne for the Landslip' in the 1930s. Along with a littering of tank traps, (including the awesome sounding 'dragons teeth') and pill boxes, the line suffered the indignity in 1940 of having its nameboards removed, in an effort to confuse invading forces. Restoration of the boards left the station named simply 'Combpyne'. Milk churns (the only method of supplying drinking water) await replacement on the platform edge.
Lens of Sutton

'Radial' tank No. 30583 heading for Axminster on 24th May 1957. The spare ground on the right was formerly occupied by a run round loop and siding but, following alterations around 1930, which included new platform facings in concrete from the Exmouth Junction works, it was taken out of use and subsequently removed.
Tony Wright

An Axminster branch train arrives at the diminutive Combpyne station in the early 'sixties.   *K. A. Stone*

An 'up' train awaiting departure on 11th April 1959. Combpyne's porter is ready with the station's elderly handcart (at least thirty years old by this time) for the day's water supply. A camping coach, for years a feature at Combpyne, stands in the siding.   *A. E. Bennett*

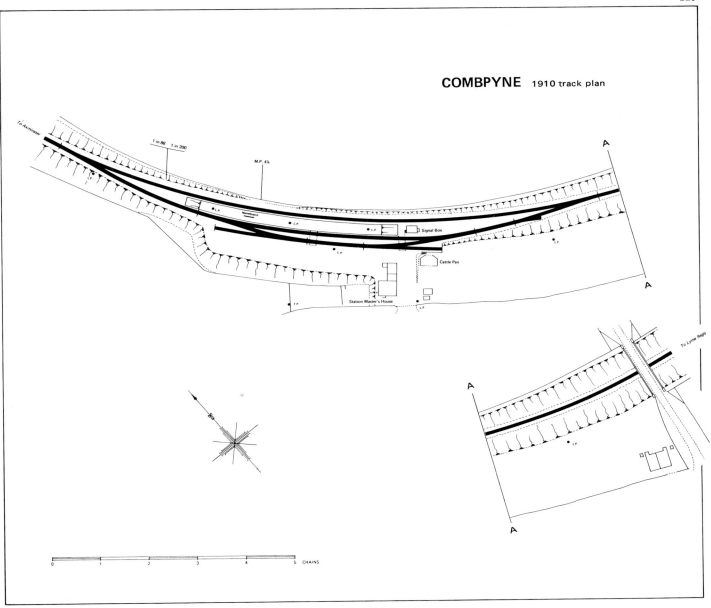

COMBPYNE 1910 track plan

To Axminster

1 in 88   1 in 200

M.P. 4¼

L.P

Nameboard

L.P

L.P

Signal Box

L.P

Cattle Pen

T.P

T.P

Station Master's House

L.P

A

A

A

A

To Lyme Regis

T.P

0   1   2   3   4   5   CHAINS

Combpyne signal box in its after-life served for many years on a local farm; first as a corn store, then as a chicken coop. It had stood by the ramp at the Lyme end of Combpyne platform. The downgrading in 1930 enabled the SR to staff the station with only a porter, ending the posts of station master and signalman. The box was identical to the one at Lyme and had a similar frame, fourteen levers with ten spare. It was replaced by a ground frame, operated by a key from the train staff.   *E. Crawforth*

Combpyne shortly after its 1930 improvements, a view which emphasizes the station's relative isolation.   *Lens of Sutton*

Although Combpyne platform was bare and without shelter, facilities at the station building were, for a sparsely inhabited district of farms and a few houses, relatively extravagant. In addition to the station master's residence, it somehow contrived to include ladies' and gents' toilets, a ticket office and a waiting room.   *R. C. Riley*

The waiting room and ticket office, on 16th August 1958.
                    A. E. West

No. 30582 departs for Lyme Regis on 14th June 1949. Freight services were not withdrawn from the line until February 1964 but traffic, never heavy, was very sparse by this time, usually odd wagon loads of coal, bricks, fertilizer, etc. In earlier years such traffic was attached to ordinary branch services more or less when required. In latter years a single mixed train more than sufficed, any wagons at Combpyne being collected by a 'down' train. In 1908, of nine trains each way daily, only five were solely for passengers and two goods only, the remainder being 'mixed'.

S. C. Nash

Combpyne dozes, framed by the loading gauge, on 20th August 1955. It remained in this somnolent state throughout its existence and hopes, like the ones expressed below, for increased traffic, were never realized: 'At present there is scarcely any population hereabouts except at Rousden, the beautiful cliff estate of Sir Wilfrid Peek; but there is excellent scope for the development of accommodation for visitors, the site being an ideal one for the erection of a hydropathic establishment or residential hotel.'

A. E. West

126

The summit of the line, nearly 500 ft above sea level, immediately beyond the platform at Combpyne. The line dropped after this through a cutting at 1 in 40 almost to Cannington Viaduct (5 miles 21 chains).   *A. E. West*

'Radial' tank No. 30583 passing under the small road bridge, south of Combpyne station, bound for the main line at Axminster in July 1952.
Edwin Course

The chalk downland rose abruptly from the sea at Lyme and, despite the steep grades, earthworks on the branch were necessarily extensive. 'Radial' tank No. 30582 passes through one of the deepest cuttings, south of Combpyne, on 14th June 1949.   *S. C. Nash*

The approach to Cannington Viaduct, from the cab of a diesel car, on 19th May 1965.   *J. E. Gready*

Cannington Viaduct, 'designated by the name of Cannington Valley', on 20th June 1959. The splendid structure fortunately survived closure and continues to grace this delightful valley.

W. Potter

A summer Saturday Axminster-Lyme train descending towards Cannington Viaduct on 14th June 1958.　　　*W. Potter*

Its elegance marred somewhat by the 'jack arch', Cannington Viaduct nevertheless provided a fine spectacle; views from passing trains were even more rewarding.

K. A. Stone

No. 30584 on the 3.55 p.m. from Lyme on 13th June 1949. The distortion of the viaduct, a consequence of 'shifting quicksands' (a description employing considerable geological licence) is dramatically apparent. *Collection J. Scrace*

An iron girder bridge carrying the branch over a small lane near Uplyme on 13th December 1965. *A. E. West*

LYME REGIS

Lyme in October 1903 with a hint of the scenery which the contemporary *Railway Magazine* correspondent found so striking: 'The scenery of the place is undeniably attractive; indeed, it would be difficult to find anywhere on the South Coast a finer range of beautiful scenery than that of which Lyme is the centre. Jane Austen compared it to the Isle of Wight, and there is undoubtedly much in common between Lyme and Ventnor, as regards both scenery and climate. As a winter residence for invalids, Lyme should rapidly grow in favour now that the drawback of a six-mile drive from the railway has been removed.'

One of the line's redoubtable pair of 'Terriers' waits with a mixed train for Axminster, some of its patrons having no doubt arrived by cab, the horse now enjoying a well earned break. The distance steeply uphill from the town was a lasting and ultimately fatal inconvenience which in 1903, it was felt, deserved some kind of explanation, if not apology: 'No attempt is made to get down to the sea level, which, as anyone acquainted with Lyme Regis knows, would have been an impossible feat for a railway worked in the ordinary way by ordinary locomotives. In explanation of our use of the word 'impossible', let us explain that the principal street in Lyme Regis rises very abruptly from the sea, and near the summit of this, at a distance of about half a mile from the centre of the place and a height of 250ft from the shore, the railway terminus has been erected.'   *Collection E. Crawforth*

'O2' 0—4—4T No. 184 prepares to leave Lyme. Adams 4—4—2Ts had largely taken over branch duties by 1914 but the less successful 'O2's (with tanks half filled to reduce weight) were still to be found on some workings. The 'Lyme Regis for Charmouth' nameboard (with attendant boulder) suffered a fate similar to that at Combpyne, reappearing after the war as simply 'Lyme Regis'. The postcard from which this view is taken was posted in September 1920 by a pioneer railway enthusiast. Here are his comments to his son: 'Here is the station, which of course I have visited — it is nearly a mile inland and you have to climb uphill from the sea 250 feet! It's a 'horrible drag'. A single line worked by 1 engine (Atlantic tank).'   *Collection C. Chivers*

'O2' No. 227 at Lyme in 1907, train and station staff lined up in familiar fashion. The station extension, again in timber and attached to the gentlemen's toilet, had appeared by now and served as a store. *Collection R. Randell*

The station on 14th May 1964, the end window by now having disappeared. *A. E. West*

Shortly after the war the Southern embarked on a series of alterations at Lyme, lengthening the building and providing an entirely new roof. The whole building was also re-clad, making a programme extensive enough to be termed 're-building'. *A. E. West*

A spring day at Lyme in 1964, the striking conifer now firmly established in the station yard. *J. E. Gready*

'Radial' No. 30583 running round its train after arriving from Axminster on 14th July 1960. *R. C. Riley*

As summer progressed, even the terminus itself at Lyme took on a distinctly wooded character, mature growth that swayed in a sea breeze. No. 30582 is featured here with the 12.33 p.m. from Axminster on 28th July 1960. *F. Church, courtesy E. Course*

The station on 27th July 1964, the paintwork still in Southern style, cream and green. *A. E. West*

Attendant with the 1930 alterations at Combpyne, new platform facings and metalled surfaces were provided at Lyme Regis. The coach is a through London vehicle, parked in the bay when not in use.
Lens of Sutton

Relaxed optimism at Lyme Regis.

Lens of Sutton

As part of the refurbishment in 1930, the platforms at Lyme were lengthened, to cope with summer Saturday five-coach trains.
D. Thompson

The goods yard handled a variety of produce, the most lucrative and long-lived being coal. Beyond the coal pens is the Lyme Regis dormitory coach, a '12-wheeler' sleeper of LNWR parentage. A number of its sisters were used in a similar capacity at Seaton, Wadebridge, Launceston and Bude. *A. E. West*

'Radial' No. E520 gliding past the goods shed in 1929. This building was unceremoniously dragged to this position during alterations to the layout in the early years.
R. Carpenter

The goods shed on 15th August 1959. In the last years, staff on lodging turns slept in the cabin attached to the goods shed. A great coal fire stove stood in one corner of the dormitory with bunks to sleep three; the palliasse covers and pillow cases were obtained from the station porter. Cooking was often carried out using these facilities but some staff opted for a fish and chip supper in the town with a 'pint in the Victoria before turning in'.

A. E. West

No. 3420 shunts a road van in Southern days, having left its train alongside the platform. Vans or wagons would normally leave as part of a mixed train.

F. Foote, courtesy R. C. Riley

Further shunting at Lyme on 31st July 1960.

K. A. Stone

The loading gauge and yard crane
c.1930.   *H.M.R.S.*

A later view of the 15 cwt crane on 17th July 1955.
Freight traffic declined to a trickle in later years but
at one time was very heavy, with the crane in frequent
use. The railway captured much of the former seaborne
trade and by 1910 over 8,000 tons of coal and
merchandise with 19,428 parcels were carried over the
line.

A. E. West

No. 30584 about to start an Axminster train on 2nd August 1959.   *K. A. Stone*

The vast output of Exmouth Junction concrete works penetrated every corner of the Southern, new platform facing being a typical standardized product. The original cattle pen was also replaced, using concrete posts.   *A. E. West*

No. 30582 trundles wearily into Lyme in the 1950s. Despite ancient stock, dating back to the 'thirties and far beyond, punctuality and reliability remained generally excellent.
     M. E. J. Deane

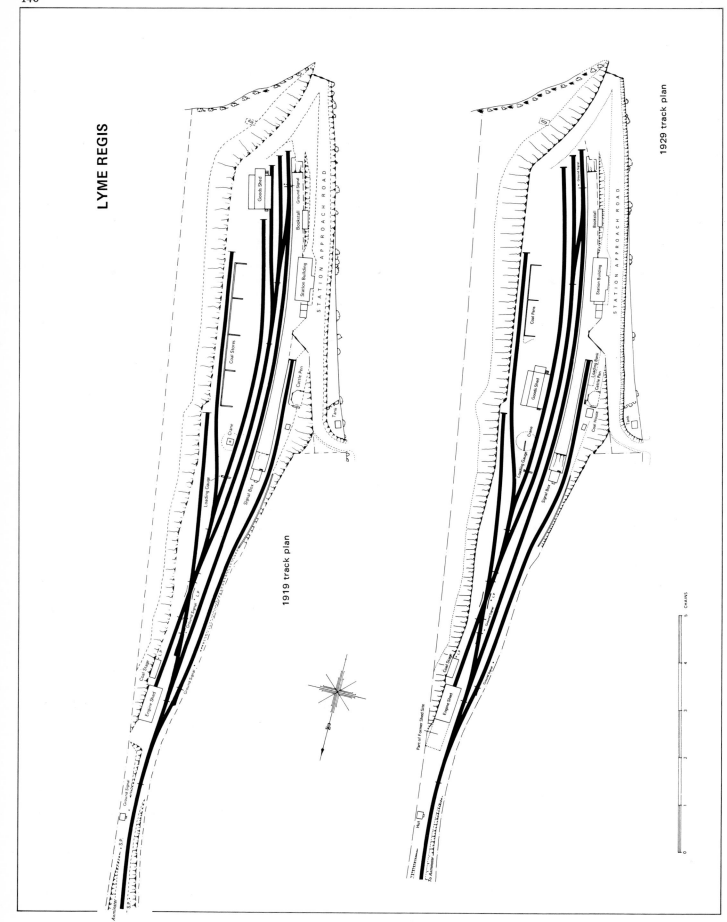

LYME REGIS

1919 track plan

1929 track plan

CHAINS

The chalkland surround at Lyme, emphasizing the station's lonely position. The wooded hills were responsible for much of the line's charm — woodland views with carpets of bluebells and primroses. The daunting gradients and wild curves were a rather less attractive aspect: 'The chain of hills surrounding the town, no point of which is less than 450 ft. above sea level, has been surmounted without recourse to a tunnel, which from the nature of the soil composing the hills might have entailed much difficulty and an indefinite expense.' The scenic rewards were probably greatest, however, on entry to the station. From cuttings and woods the passenger was suddenly presented with the wide sweep of Lyme Bay. Lewis Cozens enthusing in 1952: 'From the station superb views are obtainable to the east, stretching from the great fossil-bearing cliff of Black Ven (between Lyme Regis and Charmouth) past Golden Cap (619 feet: the highest cliff on the south coast of England) onwards by the curving Chesil Beach to distant Portland Bill, with the English Channel to complete the picture.' *M. E. J. Deane*

The signal box at Lyme was more or less identical to that at Combpyne. The frames were also to the same design, though at Lyme only one lever was spare. The box in addition housed the apparatus for the branch token, installed by the LSWR when the line was signalled. The instrument was subsequently removed and for convenience replaced in the booking office, enabling the signalman to assist in other duties about the station. The wooden sign subsequently gave way to a BR enamel version, affixed on the Axminster end. The starting signal shown in the lower left view is a conventional LSW lattice type with lower quadrant operation. By the mid 'fifties an upper quadrant arm had been fitted.
H.M.R.S. and A. E. West

A branch train heads back for Axminster in early BR days. *Authors' collection*

No. 30583 runs into Lyme past the engine shed, on 24th May 1957. The original shed, built in wood and twice the length of this building, stood on the same site until all but destroyed by fire, reportedly around 1907. Only swift action by staff prevented serious damage to a locomotive inside. Chastened by this event, the LSW had the shed rebuilt with asbestos sheeting over a steel frame. Costing over £400, it was eventually brought into use in 1913. The sleeper coal stage remained unaltered over the years, though the Southern replaced the original water column. *T. Wright*

The building in Southern days, giving more the appearance of a decrepit barn than an engine shed.
H.M.R.S.

There was a general 'tidying up' at Lyme in 1947, the neediest recipient being the shed. The doors and windows were repainted and missing portions of the cladding replaced.
L. & G.R.P.
courtesy David & Charles

Shed chores at Lyme in July 1960. Following its long overdue (possibly its only) refurbishment, the shed foundations promptly shifted. A sub shed of Exmouth Junction, it nevertheless remained officially in use until the end of steam.
K. A. Stone

No. 30582 at the appropriately named Uplyme, climbs doggedly away from the coast with the 12.29 'up' train on 14th June 1949. A memorable journey on an extraordinary line awaited the occupants of the single coach.

Collection J. Scrace

A final look at the terminus, occupied, as on many occasions in the last years, by an enthusiasts' special. Following a period of dereliction, the station building has happily found a new lease of life on the Mid Hants Railway, as a book and model shop.　　*Lens of Sutton*

LYME REGIS BRANCH.

WEEKDAYS — Will not apply on SATURDAYS, 28th MAY to 24th SEPTEMBER, 1949.

m. c.	DOWN		a.m.		A a.m.	p.m.	p.m.		p.m.		p.m.		p.m.		p.m.	p.m.	p.m.	A
0 0	Axminster	⊤	8 35		10 43	12 2	1 5	...	2 0	...	2 55	...	4 43		5 40	6 44	7 55	8 55
4 21	Combpyne		8 48		10 56	12 15	1 18		2 13		3 8		4 56		5 53	6 57	8 8	9 8
6 59	Lyme Regis	⊤	8 55½		11 3½	12 22½	1 25½		2 20½		3 15½		5 3½		6 0½	7 4½	8 15½	9 15½

m. c.	UP		a.m.		a.m.	a.m.		p.m.	p.m.		p.m.		A p.m.	p.m.		p.m.	p.m.	p.m.
0 0	Lyme Regis	⊤	8 4		10 0	11 34	...	12 29	1 31	...	2 26	...	4 0	5 10	...	6 7	7 20	8 22
2 38	Combpyne		8 12½		10 8½	11 42½		12 37½	1 39½		2 34½		4 8½	5 18½		6 15½	7 28½	8 30½
6 59	Axminster	⊤	8 25		10 21	11 55		12 50	1 52		2 47		4 21	5 31		6 28	7 41	8 43

SATURDAYS ONLY, 28th MAY to 24th SEPTEMBER, 1949.

DOWN	a.m.	a.m.	a.m.	a.m.		p.m.		p.m.		p.m.		p.m.	p.m.		p.m.	p.m.	p.m.
Axminster	8 32	9 30	10 30	11 30	...	12 30	...	1 45	...	3 20	...	4 43	5 40	...	6 50	7 55	8 55
Combpyne	8 45	9 43	10 43	11 43		12 43		1 58		3 33		4 56	5 53		7 3	8 8	9 8
Lyme Regis	8 52½	9 50½	10 50½	11 59½		12 50½		2 5½		3 40½		5 3½	6 0½		7 10½	8 15½	9 15½

UP	a.m.	a.m.	a.m.	a.m.		noon		p.m.		p.m.		p.m.		p.m.	p.m.	p.m.	p.m.
Lyme Regis	8 0	9 0	10 0	11 0	...	12 0	...	1 10	...	2 40	...	3 55	...	5 10	6 7	7 20	8 22
Combpyne	8 8½	9 8½	10 8½	11 8½		12 8½		1 18½		2 48½		4 3½		5 18½	6 15½	7 28½	8 30½
Axminster	8 21	9 21	10 21	11 21		12 21		1 31		3 1		4 16		5 31	6 28	7 41	8 43

SUNDAYS.

DOWN	a.m.	Excn. DF p.m.		E p.m.		D p.m.		p.m.		p.m.		D p.m.		CD p.m.		D p.m.	Excn. DF p.m.
Axminster	11 11	12 6	...	12 40	...	1 0	...	3 10	...	4 25	...	5 50	...	7 33	...	8 30	10 20
Combpyne	11 24	12 19		12 53		1 13		3 23		4 38		6 3		7 46		8 43	10 33
Lyme Regis	11 31½	12 26½		1 0½		1 20½		3 30½		4 45½		6 10½		7 53½		8 50½	10 40½

UP	a.m.		a.m.		Excn. DF p.m.		p.m.		p.m.		D p.m.		D p.m.		D p.m.		Excn. DF p.m.
Lyme Regis	10 40	...	11 37	...	12 35	...	2 35	...	3 55	...	5 10	...	7 0	...	7 58	...	9 50
Combpyne	10 48½		11 45½		12 41½		2 43½		4 3½		5 18½		7 8½		8 6½		9 58½
Axminster	11 1		11 58		12 54		2 56		4 16		5 31		7 21		8 18½		10 11

A—Runs as Mixed Train when required.　C—Not to be held for 4.5 p.m. Q from Waterloo.　D—Will run until 25th September only.
E　Commences 2nd October, and run 10 minutes later when 12.12 p.m. Q Pass. Exeter Central to Waterloo runs.
F　Available for ordinary passengers.

'Radial' tank, archetypal Lyme Regis loco, and responsible more than most other factors for the affection and interest lavished on the line over the years. No. 3125 of the renowned trio is pictured at Axminster on 16th September 1936.

H. C. Casserley

One of the 'Radials' ill-fated replacements, ex-LBSC 'D1' 0—4—2T No. B359, on 4th May 1930.

H. C. Casserley

LOCOMOTIVES & OPERATIONAL NOTES

The branch became synonymous of course with the Adams 'Radial' 4—4—2Ts and they indeed dominated the line for many years. The locomotive history is well known, having appeared on a number of occasions. It will suffice to summarize it here.

The first loco was No. 131, provided by the LSWR and used during construction of the line:

> The steepness of the gradients requires a powerful locomotive, and the London and South Western Railway has provided a six-wheels coupled saddle tank engine of the following dimensions: Total wheel base, 13 ft. 9 in.; grate area, 14 square feet; cylinders, 17 in. diameter; stroke, 24 in.; weight, in working order, 31 tons 19 cwts. 2 qr.; tractive force on rails, 10,880 lbs.

The saddle tanks proved less than successful and a pair of ex-LBSCR 'Terriers' Nos. 734 and 735 (646 *Newington* and 668 *Clapham* respectively) arrived in time for the opening day ceremonies. Hard working on the tight curves overtaxed the little 0—6—0Ts and, after deputizing on numerous occasions, 'O2' 0—4—4Ts finally took over in 1907.

Despite reduced weight, etc., including partly filled tanks, the problems that had bedevilled the 'Terriers' persisted: strained frames, excessive flange wear and sundry steam and water leaks. Someone thought the elderly Adams 4—4—Ts might be worthwhile, at least as a temporary measure and three were regularly employed by 1914.

The first, No. 0125 of 1885, remained on the Lyme Regis branch, eventually to be joined by No. 0520 in 1926. No. 0520 had in fact replaced 521 in August 1925 and 0419 had left in November 1923. Emergencies, etc.

Of the four 'D1' 0—4—2Ts turned out for the branch, only to be replaced by the refurbished 'Radials', No. B633 was retained at Exmouth Junction, ostensibly the 'spare' engine.

R. C. Riley

No description of the Lyme Regis branch would be complete without some portrait of a 'Radial' tank. The class were originally constructed between 1882 and 1885, totalling over seventy. The magnificent No. 3520 was one of two retained at work by the Southern, the third prodigal, of course, returning 'home' via Government service and the East Kent Railway.

Collection E. Crawforth
and F. Foote, courtesy R. C. Riley

were covered by Exmouth Junction 'O2's until modified ex-LBSCR 'D1' 0—4—2Ts arrived in 1928, the Adams tanks being removed ostensibly for scrap. Trials with an ex-SECR 'P' 0—6—0T No. A558 had proved wholly unsuccessful. Nos. B276, B359, B612 and B633, the 'D1's fared no better than the 'O2's and eventually the 4—4—2Ts, overhauled, had to be recalled. By the summer of 1930 they were both back at work on the branch as 0125 and 0520.

These stalwarts were joined by a third 'Radial' in 1946, No. 5 of the East Kent Railway, sold to the latter by the LSWR via a Government Salvage Depot in 1917. Fully overhauled, it was numbered 3488 in August 1946. All three 4—4—2Ts continued work through to the 'sixties as Nos. 30582 (ex-3125), 30583 (ex-3488) and 30584 (ex-3520), when a further series of 'trials' took place. Tentative electrification proposals of the mid 'fifties were soon dismissed and in 1958 an ex-GWR '1400' class 0—4—2T, No. 1462, proved itself unsuccessful. In September 1960 an Ivatt 2—6—2T of LMS design, No. 41297, was tried, apparently with rather better results.

Similar tests followed with sister engine No. 41308 and in January 1961 No. 30584 was withdrawn. The other two 4—4—2Ts followed five months later. In 1965 the Ivatt 2—6—2 tanks returned, deputizing for diesel cars the latter having been introduced in November 1963.

Two former Lyme Regis engines are now preserved. 'Terrier' No. 734 was sold to the Freshwater, Yarmouth and Newport Railway in 1913, becoming FYNR No. 2. Under the auspices of the Southern Railway it acquired number W8. British Rail renumbered the loco 32646 in August 1949 and it is now in service at Haven Street, I.O.W. Adams 'Radial' No. 30583 (3488), having recently been refurbished in BR livery, sees regular service on the Bluebell Railway in Sussex.

Ex-GWR 0—4—2T No. 1462 runs into Lyme Regis whilst undergoing trials on 12th November 1958.   *S. C. Nash*

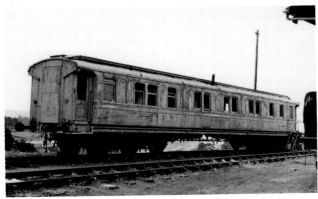
Lyme Regis sleeping accommodation (described elsewhere).
                J. H. Lucking

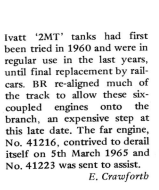
Ivatt '2MT' tanks had first been tried in 1960 and were in regular use in the last years, until final replacement by railcars. BR re-aligned much of the track to allow these six-coupled engines onto the branch, an expensive step at this late date. The far engine, No. 41216, contrived to derail itself on 5th March 1965 and No. 41223 was sent to assist.
                E. Crawforth

LYME REGIS STATION BUILDING

F O R E C O U R T   E L E V A T I O N

E L E V A T I O N   T O   P L A T F O R M

E N D   E L E V A T I O N

SCALE — 2 mm to 1 foot

LYME REGIS SIGNAL BOX

F R O N T   E L E V A T I O N

E N D   E L E V A T I O N

R E A R   E L E V A T I O N

E N D   E L E V A T I O N

SCALE — 2 mm to 1 foot

LYME REGIS GOODS SHED

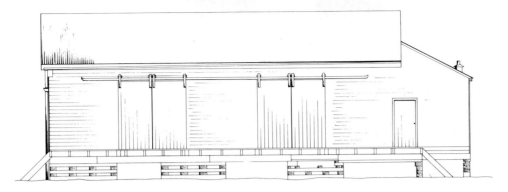

E L E V A T I O N   T O   R A I L S

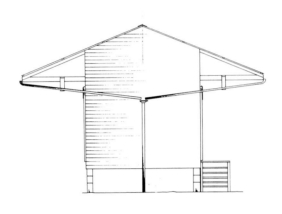

E N D   E L E V A T I O N

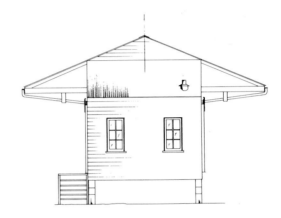

E N D   E L E V A T I O N

SCALE — 2 mm to 1 foot

The goods shed in 1963. The bins contained water treatment brickettes for locomotive use.   *A. E. West*

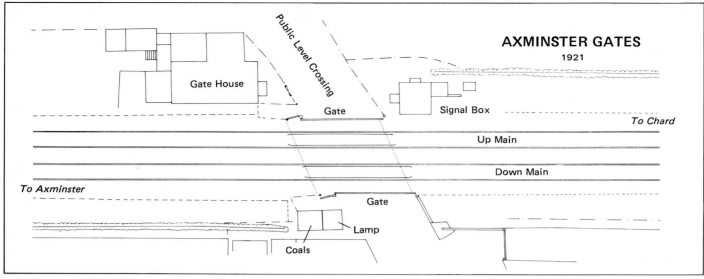

AXMINSTER GATES
1921

Public Level Crossing

Gate House

Gate

Signal Box

To Chard

Up Main

Down Main

To Axminster

Gate

Lamp

Coals

'Axminster Gates', some 200 yards east of the station, on 21st January 1966. The wicket gates were ordered in 1921 at a cost of £53 accompanied by 'unclimbable iron fencing'. To the left of the box is the former gatehouse. Axminster Gates closed completely on 16th December 1975 when automatic barriers were installed. Of note in latter years was the creation of a block post, after Axminster signal box had closed, in March 1967. Its upgrading was short-lived, however, the line being singled in June that year.
E. Crawforth

ACKNOWLEDGEMENTS

We would like to express our warmest thanks to those without whom Volume Two of *Branch Lines of the Southern Railway* would never have seen completion. A number we suspect might very well have given up hope altogether of ever seeing it published — we hope it will be a pleasant surprise!

Ted ('Smokey') Crawforth, one time fireman on the Lyme Regis branch, somehow kept faith. He has spent many hours adding information and correcting the Lyme Regis section and the book owes much to his expert knowledge. To him and his wife Freda we express our warmest thanks and appreciation. John Wimble showed enormous kindness in making all his New Romney notes and material available and continued to render enthusiastic assistance throughout Volume Two's lengthy gestation. Others who gave generously of their time, providing inestimable help and encouragement, included Colin Chivers (of the South Western Circle), Hubert Wheeller and Mr. A. E. West, the latter two gentlemen having an intimate and lengthy association with the Epsom Downs and Lyme Regis branches respectively. The Epsom Downs operational notes are in the main the work of Mr. Wheeller. Peter Carey was of especial help regarding the New Romney line and Mr. D. G. Halliday kindly provided plans and material from his collection. Dick Riley once again exerted a gently corrective influence; to him our warmest thanks. We would also like to acknowledge the help of the South Western Circle for the use of Lyme Regis drawings in that society's possession, and to Mr. A. F. J. Kerr who drew the originals. Derek Brough, John Scrace and Sid Nash were kind enough to spend time reading the proofs and added very useful and constructive information. To them our sincere thanks.

We would also like to thank the following long-suffering photographers, organizations, colleagues, friends and well-wishers: Edwin Course; Ivo Peters; George Barlow; the Romney Hythe and Dymchurch Railway; Folkestone Library; George Hookham; Reg Randell (what can we say?); Tony Riley; Alan. A. Jackson; David Wallis; Mrs. Wallis (special thanks for the use of her late husband's photographs); Mr. M. Caulfield, B.Sc., I.C. (our thanks and of course congratulations); New Romney Library; Dick Orpwood; Ian Rivers and John Minnis of the Brighton Circle; Mr. R. F. Roberts, who had the unique presence of mind to visit 'the Marsh' in July 1937; Mr. J. Spencer-Gilks; Derek Clayton; Sutton Library, in particular June Braunton; Dave Newman; Banstead Library; Peter Tangye; Eddie Wilmshurst; Tony Wright; and — what would we do without him? — Chris Turner; the Locomotive Club of Great Britain for the use of the Ken Nunn collection; Nigel Hearn (special thanks); H. C. Casserley; R. T. H. Platt; David & Charles for the use of L & GRP photos; Dr. I. C. Allen; Douglas Thompson; H. A. Vallance; S. W. Baker; Roger Carpenter; W. A. Camwell; K. A. Stone; W. Potter; M. E. J. Deane; J. E. Gready; A. E. Bennett; F. Church; F. Foote; the Historical Model Railway Society; B. Cope and J. H. Lucking.

To those longest and closest associated with the book, BR staff at Waterloo and Croydon, we can only give thanks yet again, in the knowledge that it would have been wholly impossible without their interest and knowledge.

It remains only to thank June Judge and Paul Karau for production work on the book, accomplished with a grimmer than usual determination and an ability to smile at almost anything, even ingrate authors. Of course, to Beverly and Wendy, who typed and retyped the usual endless succession of amendments, corrections and additions, the warmest thanks of all.